Shih Tzu

2nd Edition

GET MORE!
Visit www.wiley.com/
go/shih_tzu

Jo Ann White

Howell
Book House™

Copyright © 2005 by Wiley Publishing, Inc., Hoboken, New Jersey. All rights reserved.

Howell Book House
Published by Wiley Publishing, Inc., Hoboken, New Jersey

For general information on our other products and services or to obtain technical support please contact our Customer Care Department within the U.S. at (800) 762-2974, outside the U.S. at (317) 572-3993 or fax (317) 572-4002.

Wiley also publishes its books in a variety of electronic formats. Some content that appears in print may not be available in electronic books. For more information about Wiley products, please visit our web site at www.wiley.com.

Library of Congress Cataloging-in-Publication Data:
White, Jo Ann, date.
    Shih Tzu/Jo Ann White—2nd ed.
      p. cm—(Your happy healthy pet)
    ISBN-13: 978-0-7645-8384-1 (cloth: alk. paper)
    ISBN-10: 0-7645-8384-0 (cloth: alk. paper)
    1. Shih Tzu. I. Title. II. Series.
SF429.S64W48   2005
636.76—dc22
                                                                          2005002072

Printed in the United States of America

10   9   8   7   6   5   4   3

2nd Edition

Book design by Melissa Auciello-Brogan
Cover design by Michael J. Freeland
Illustrations in chapter 9 by Shelley Norris and Karl Brandt
Book production by Wiley Publishing, Inc. Composition Services

About the Author

Jo Ann White acquired her first Shih Tzu in 1967, before the breed was officially recognized by the American Kennel Club. Thus began her ongoing love affair with this delightful breed. Her first champion, who did not want to stop going to dog shows when she retired from the conformation ring, became the first Shih Tzu bitch in the United States to earn both a show championship and an obedience title.

Jo Ann has bred and/or owned about twenty champions and several obedience titlists under her Heavenly Dynasty kennel name. She is the former president of the American Shih Tzu Club, which awarded her a lifetime membership for extraordinary service to the breed in 2004, and is vice president of the Shih Tzu Fanciers of Central Florida.

Jo Ann is the author of several other books, including *The Official Book of the Shih Tzu*, and numerous magazine articles about dogs. She has been the Shih Tzu breed columnist for the *AKC Gazette* since 1988. A freelance reference book writer and editor with particular interest in the Third World, she now lives on the Gulf Coast of Florida with two retired and very spoiled Shih Tzu. Many of the photographs in this book were taken by her late husband, Richard Lawall.

About Howell Book House

Since 1961, Howell Book House has been America's premier publisher of pet books. We're dedicated to companion animals and the people who love them, and our books reflect that commitment. Our stable of authors—training experts, veterinarians, breeders, and other authorities—is second to none. And we've won more Maxwell Awards from the Dog Writers Association of America than any other publisher.

As we head toward the half-century mark, we're more committed than ever to providing new and innovative books, along with the classics our readers have grown to love. This year, we're launching several exciting new initiatives, including redesigning the Howell Book House logo and revamping our biggest pet series, Your Happy Healthy Pet™, with bold new covers and updated content. From bringing home a new puppy to competing in advanced equestrian events, Howell has the titles that keep animal lovers coming back again and again.

Contents

Shopping List

You'll need to do a bit of stocking up before you bring your new dog or puppy home. Below is a basic list of some must-have supplies. For more detailed information on the selection of each item below, consult Chapter 5. For specific guidance on what grooming tools you'll need, review Chapter 7.

☐ Food dish   ☐ Nail clippers

☐ Water dish   ☐ Grooming tools

☐ Dog food   ☐ Chew toys

☐ Leash   ☐ Toys

☐ Collar   ☐ ID tag

☐ Crate

There are likely to be a few other items that you're dying to pick up before bringing your dog home. Use the following blanks to note any additional items you'll be shopping for.

☐ _____

☐ _____

☐ _____

☐ _____

☐ _____

☐ _____

☐ _____

☐ _____

☐ _____

☐ _____

☐ _____

☐ _____

Pet Sitter's Guide

We can be reached at (___)_____-_____ Cellphone (___)_____-_____

We will return on _____ (date) at _____ (approximate time)

Dog's Name _____

Breed, Age, and Sex _____

Important Names and Numbers

Vet's Name _____ Phone (___)_____- _____

Address_____

Emergency Vet's Name _____ Phone (___)_____- _____

Address_____

Poison Control _____ (or call vet first)

Other individual to contact in case of emergency _____

_____

Care Instructions

In the following three blanks let the sitter know what to feed, how much, and when; when the dog should go out; when to give treats; and when to exercise the dog.

Morning_____

_____

Afternoon_____

_____

Evening _____

_____

Medications needed (dosage and schedule) _____

_____

Any special medical conditions _____

_____

Grooming instructions _____

_____

My dog's favorite playtime activities, quirks, and other tips_____

_____

_____

Part I
The World of the Shih Tzu

The Shih Tzu

Stop

Muzzle

Skull

Crest

Neck

Withers

Back

Shoulder

Stifle or Knee

Hock

Toes

Chapter 1

What Is a Shih Tzu?

For hundreds of years, Shih Tzu have been bred to be human companions, and their friendly, outgoing personality reflects this fact. In pre-revolutionary China, it was a status symbol to own a dog who had no utilitarian function, such as hunting or guarding. Shih Tzu were highly prized in the imperial court, where they lived lives of luxury.

Because the Shih Tzu has always been intended as a companion, in both show dogs and pet dogs the correct temperament is of the utmost importance. Shih Tzu are alert, arrogant, and affectionate. They love people and other dogs, big and small. Everyone is this breed's friend. It is most unusual and highly undesirable for a Shih Tzu to be nasty, overly aggressive, nervous, or shy.

But people love them for their looks, as well. The Shih Tzu's unique head and expression distinguish the breed from two other related Oriental breeds, the Lhasa Apso and the Pekingese. Although the Shih Tzu is classified by the American Kennel Club (AKC) as a member of the Toy Group, the dog is solid and sturdy. Many consider the Shih Tzu to be a big dog in a little package, in both temperament and substance.

The Shih Tzu breed standard describes the ideal specimen of the breed. Although the perfect dog has never been born, dog show judging is based on how closely each dog entered approaches the ideal described in the breed standard. Reputable breeders *always* try to produce dogs that conform to the AKC breed standard.

The breed standard is definitely worth reading, so you can understand exactly what type of dog the Shih Tzu is meant to be. In this chapter, I will summarize the standard and explain the important points.

What Is a Breed Standard?

A breed standard is a detailed description of the perfect dog of that breed. Breeders use the standard as a guide in their breeding programs, and judges use it to evaluate the dogs in conformation shows. The standard is written by the national breed club, using guidelines established by the registry that recognizes the breed.

The first section of the breed standard gives a brief overview of the breed's history. Then it describes the dog's general appearance and size as an adult. Next is a detailed description of the head and neck, then the back and body, and the front and rear legs. The standard then describes the ideal coat and how the dog should be presented in the show ring. It also lists all acceptable colors, patterns, and markings. Then there's a section on how the dog moves, called *gait*. Finally, there's a general description of the dog's temperament.

Each section also lists characteristics that are considered to be faults or disqualifications in the conformation ring. Superficial faults in appearance are often what distinguish a pet-quality dog from a show- or competition-quality dog. However, some faults affect the way a dog moves or his overall health. And faults in temperament are serious business.

You can read all the AKC breed standards at www.akc.org.

The Shih Tzu Head

Much of the breed standard is devoted to describing the head, because this feature most distinguishes the breed. It is sometimes difficult to determine whether head and expression are correct simply by looking at them because skilled groomers can do up a dog's topknot to make the head appear correct even when it is not.

When you think of the correct head and expression, think round, warm, and soft. The head is large and round when viewed from the front or the side, and the ears appear to blend into the head. The eyes are also large and round, but

The Shih Tzu's head is one of the most important features of the breed. Think "round, warm, soft" and you have the right idea.

thcy should not protrude. Although a small amount of eye white is acceptable, excessive eye white in the corners of the eye or around the entire eye, or bulging eyes markedly detract from the desired warm, sweet expression, as does a lack of pigmentation on the nose, lips, or eye rims. The eyes should be placed well apart, and the muzzle should be set no lower than the bottom of the eye rims.

The muzzle is short and square and unwrinkled—unlike the longer, narrower muzzle of the Lhasa Apso or the extremely short, wrinkled muzzle of the Pekingese. The muzzle should have good cushioning (fleshy padding), which contributes greatly to the soft expression.

The bite is slightly undershot—that is, the lower jaw is longer than the upper jaw. The teeth should not show when the mouth is closed and the lower lip should not protrude when viewed from the side. The muzzle meets the foreskull at a definite angle (called the stop), giving the desired "pushed-in" look.

One of the most serious head problems in a Shih Tzu is what breeders often refer to as the "Andy Gump" look. This means the head is more oval than round, and also has a combination of other faults—a narrow, long muzzle that is set too low; close-set, small eyes; a lack of stop and of cushioning on the muzzle; and a receding underjaw. Even if the jaw is not actually overshot (the upper jaw is longer than the lower jaw), the dog looks as if his muzzle is pointing downward, seems to have a weak chin, and cannot possibly have the correct expression.

A Small but Solid Dog

Good Shih Tzu are solid dogs who are surprisingly heavy for their size. Mature Shih Tzu should be slightly longer from the withers (the top of the shoulder) to the base of tail than they are high at the withers. Most Shih Tzu in today's show rings measure slightly longer than high, although a wealth of hair may make the dogs appear shorter in back than they really are. The chest is broad and deep, the ribs are well curved, and the legs are sturdy and muscular.

The standard calls for a weight range of 9 to 16 pounds. There is therefore no such thing as an officially recognized "imperial" or "tiny teacup" Shih Tzu, and historic evidence suggests that Shih Tzu in the Chinese imperial court were generally about the same size as Shih Tzu today.

Words like "teacup" are used by less reputable breeders to describe undersized Shih Tzu, often in an effort to suggest the smaller dogs are special and are therefore worth a higher price. While an ethical breeder may occasionally have a runt in a litter, this puppy is sold as a companion dog and is not used for breeding. The deliberate downsizing of an already small breed not only creates abnormally small Shih Tzu who may not be shown in the dog show ring, but also produces puppies who may have health problems. This is not indicative of an "imperial gene," but rather of poor breeding practices. If you want a really tiny dog, you should consider another breed.

What's Under All the Hair?

Although a Shih Tzu with long legs and a narrow head and body may appear to be in correct proportion due to the wealth of hair, he is not. Equally incorrect is the short-legged, barrel-chested Shih Tzu who looks dumpy and squatty. These are quite common faults, and some people think a dog who is a only a little bit incorrect in many respects is very close to the ideal. But in fact, the dog is a poor specimen of the breed and is genetically more likely to produce puppies who are also poor specimens than will a dog with only one or two faults that are more serious. As an analogy, compare the difficulty of replacing your kitchen cabinets with remodeling your entire house!

The body of the Shih Tzu is compact, with little distance between the last rib and the pelvis. You should never see the kind of tucked-up tummy found in racier breeds such as Greyhounds. In a Shih Tzu with the proper spring of rib and depth of chest, the rib cage should drop to just below the elbow. The chest should never be so wide that it forces the elbows out, nor so narrow that the dog seems to have flat sides.

Under his long coat a Shih Tzu is a sturdy little dog.

Build and Movement

Structural soundness is as important in the Shih Tzu as it is in any dog. A Shih Tzu with incorrect structure cannot possibly have the smooth, flowing, effortless movement that makes the breed so elegant and that the standard calls for.

One of the most common problems in this breed is a poorly put-together front, and that really affects the way the dog moves. The neck should flow smoothly into the shoulders, which should be set at about a 90-degree angle and fit smoothly into the body. Excessive development of muscles on the outside of the shoulder blade or shoulders that lack in the desired angulation or that protrude from the topline (the dog's outline from just behind the withers to the tail) and interrupt the smooth line from the neck to the shoulders to the withers are considered to be undesirable. The shoulder blades should lie flat and point toward the spine.

How does this affect movement? If the front shoulders and legs are too far forward, the weight-bearing muscles and shoulders will not support the head, neck, and ribs as they should and the neck will not blend smoothly into the back. The dog will take short, mincing steps rather than correctly stepping out with good reach in the front. When this incorrect movement is viewed from the side, the topline will bounce. The stress of inefficient movement will cause the dog to tire easily and have difficulty holding his head up in the correct arrogant carriage.

The front legs should be straight from the elbows to the pasterns (the area between the wrist and the foot) and set well apart to support the broad, deep chest. The elbows should be set close to the body and the feet should point straight ahead. If the front legs are bowed or out at the elbows or the dog is barrel-chested, he will appear to roll like a Pekingese when moving toward you or to swing his legs out to the side and then in, rather than extending them straight ahead. This makes for very inefficient and incorrect movement, as does turning the toes in or out.

The angulation of the shoulders and hips should be in balance for smooth movement, with the front legs reaching out well while the rear legs provide strong drive from the back. If both front and rear lack the correct angulation, the dog will move with a short, mincing stride, bobbing up and down instead of moving forward effortlessly. If the rear is more angulated than the front, the dog will sometimes move with what is called a "hackney gait," picking up his front legs excessively high to keep them out of the way of the oncoming back feet. A dog whose front and rear angulation are not in balance may also walk with a slight sideways angle (called "crabbing") rather than straight forward to avoid having his rear legs interfere with his front ones. In general, a dog whose front and rear angulation are insufficient but are in balance will look better when he is moving than one who has poor angulation in just the front or just the rear. However, that does not make him a better dog; lack of angulation at both ends involves two faults rather than just one!

The hind legs, like the front legs, should be sturdy, muscular, and set well apart in line with the front legs. The lower part of the leg (the hock) should be short enough to provide sufficient leverage for the desired strong, driving movement in the rear. In some Shih Tzu, the tendons that hold the hock joints in place may be weak, causing them to buckle forward when gentle pressure is applied to the back of the joint. This is incorrect.

Tops and Tails

When viewed from the side while moving, the Shih Tzu should have a firm, level topline, the head should be carried well up, and the tail curved gently over the back in what is called a "teacup handle." Overall balance is of the utmost importance. A too-small head atop a too-long neck is as objectionable as a too-large head atop a too-short neck. A too-long or too-short back, a back that curves up, a topline that gets higher toward the rear of the dog, and even an incorrect tail can upset the desired balance. Incorrect tailset ranges from a tail that is too loose (like a Beagle), too tight (curled like a Pug), or too flat (like a Pekingese), to a tail that is set too low at the base of the spine.

The Shih Tzu's Coat

Certainly, one distinctive feature of the Shih Tzu is the dog's long, flowing double coat, which may be slightly wavy but never curly. The

The long, flowing double coat doesn't stop this dog from jumping for joy. But it does require a lot of grooming.

double coat consists of a dense, soft undercoat, and a somewhat harder outercoat. A sparse coat or a single coat (one without the undercoat) is undesirable. Because the coat is so profuse, it requires a great deal of grooming, although a coat of the correct sturdy texture requires much less care than a soft, cottony coat, and is therefore much sought after. The coat is normally parted in the center of the back, and the hair on the top of the head is tied into a topknot.

A Rainbow of Colors

The Shih Tzu comes in a variety of colors and markings, and all colors and markings are equally acceptable according to the breed standard. Among the most common colors and combinations are gold and white, red and white, black and white, silver and white, brindle (a mixture of gold or silver and black) and white, solid gold or silver with a black mask, and solid black.

Less common are liver coats and blue coats. These two coat colors are recessive and are the result of the absence of the color gene for black. These dogs have chocolate brown or gray-blue pigment and may have lighter eyes—correct for those coat colors, although light eyes are a fault in any other color. Black tips at the ends of the hairs on the outercoat and on the ears, and black eye stripes at the outer corners of the eyes on light-colored dogs are common. In a young puppy, it is necessary to look close to the skin to see the color the dog will be when the black tips grow out.

What Is a Breed Club?

Every breed recognized by the AKC has a national breed club, sometimes called the parent club. National clubs are a great source of information about your breed. You can get the name of the current club secretary from the AKC web site (www.akc.org) or the web site of the American Shih Tzu Club (www.shihtzu.org), which provides great information about the breed and contacts for breeder referral, Shih Tzu rescue, and local Shih Tzu breed clubs throughout the United States.

There are also numerous all-breed, individual breed, obedience, sporting, and other special-interest dog clubs across the country. The AKC can provide you with a geographical list of clubs to find ones in your area, and you can get information about dog shows scheduled to be held near you at www.infodog.com.

It is not unusual for Shih Tzu to change color as they mature. Red may fade to gold and gold to cream. Silver may darken to deep charcoal over time. Some judges unfortunately place too much emphasis on flashy markings or colors, but the breed standard clearly states that color and markings are totally irrelevant in terms of quality.

What the Standard Means for You

If you have purchased a pet Shih Tzu, chances are the dog possesses one or more faults based on the breed standard that make him unsuitable for the show ring or for breeding. That doesn't mean he's not a great pet—just that he's not a show dog.

Most breeders are unwilling to sell an excellent show prospect to a home where the dog will not be shown. In many cases, however, the faults your dog has may be obvious only to someone involved in the show world and you will not even notice them. If you later decide you would like to buy a show- or breeding-quality Shih Tzu, you should read every book and watch every video on the breed you can, attend dog shows, and talk to reputable breeders.

Being familiar with the breed standard will help you find a reputable breeder and accurately judge whether your dog is a show prospect or just a super pet.

Meanwhile, a thorough knowledge of the breed standard will enable you to understand why you should spay or neuter your pet rather than allow these faults to be reproduced, and will help you recognize a good example of the breed. And your dog can still compete in all kinds of canine sports, entertain you and your friends, be your best pal, or even be a registered therapy dog and bring the same joy to others that he brings to you.

Whether or not your pet is an excellent representative according to the breed standard, he can still be an ideal companion and house pet. That is, after all, what Shih Tzu were bred for and why you want one. Your dog will—and should—always be Best in Show in your eyes!

Famous Shih Tzu Owners

Yul Brynner

Mariah Carey

Phyllis Diller

Zsa Zsa Gabor

Bill Gates

The Dalai Lama

Greg Maddux

Chapter 2

The Shih Tzu's Ancestors

The Shih Tzu is one of several types of lion dogs whose ancestors developed in Asia at least as long ago as the year 1000. These breeds include the Shih Tzu, Lhasa Apso, Pug, and Japanese Chin. The ancestors of the modern Shih Tzu may have been introduced to China from Tibet or Central Asia. Whatever their origin, our so-called chrysanthemum-faced breed had an honored place in the Chinese imperial court, particularly during the Manchu Dynasty (1644–1911).

Breeding of palace dogs was done by court eunuchs, and particular colors and patterns of markings were carefully sought and described in flowery prose. A dog with a black body, white belly, and white feet, for example, was described as "black clouds over snow," whereas one with a gold coat and a white dome was a "golden basin upholding the moon."

Little Lion Dogs

The name Shih Tzu (pronounced *sheet-zoo*) means "lion" in Chinese. Ancient scroll paintings show short-legged dogs trimmed to resemble lions, with heavily bearded and mustached faces. The breed's lion-like appearance gave it particular symbolic importance. In Tibetan Buddhism, the lion is Buddha's steed and most important companion, and is therefore sacred.

Lions are not indigenous to the Far East, however, so lion-like dogs took their place in religious significance. Huge stone lion dogs guarded many temples and public buildings. Among its attributes, the Chinese said that the lion dog should have dragon eyes, a lion head, a bear torso, a frog mouth, palm-leaf fan ears, a feather-duster tail, and movement like a goldfish. Many of these lion dogs were presented in pairs, with the male resting his front feet on a ball and the female resting her foot on a puppy. Often they wore harnesses ornamented with tassels and bells, and held ropes or ribbons in their mouths.

Lion dogs were depicted on painted scrolls, and lion dog statues were placed on household altars and ornamented the roof corners of temples, where they were thought to protect the temples from fire. Some of these lion dogs are shown being ridden by Siddhartha Gautama, the founder of Buddhism, or by the Bodhisattva Manjusri, who was said to be accompanied by a pet dog who could transform itself into a lion.

As this porcelain figure shows, male little lion dogs were often portrayed with their front feet resting on a ball.

Representations of lion dogs (also known as Foo or Fu dogs and collected by many Shih Tzu owners) appear not only in Chinese art, but also in the art of Tibet, Japan, Korea, Thailand, and Indonesia. Unlike the ferocious lion, the lion dogs are often smiling. Perhaps they reflect the ancient Shih Tzu's arrogant bearing and affectionate personality—or perhaps these attributes were selectively bred for long ago because of the breed's importance as both a religious symbol and a treasured companion.

Out of the Far East

After the fall of the Manchu Dynasty in 1911, Shih Tzu continued to be bred outside the imperial palace by Chinese and foreigners. At this time, the various Tibetan breeds were known collectively to Westerners as Tibetan or Lhasa Lion Dogs. The first Shih Tzu were taken from China to the West in the late 1920s and early 1930s. Without these early exports, we would have no Shih Tzu today.

The breed is believed to have disappeared in China after the Communists came to power in 1949, because pet dogs were considered to be a symbol of wealth and privilege and a drain on scarce resources. All of today's Shih Tzu are descended from thirteen dogs exported to England, Ireland, Norway, and

Shih Tzu and their owners at a dog show in Britain in 1933.

Sweden from China and a purebred black and white Pekingese who was bred to a Shih Tzu in England by Elfreda Evans in 1952. This controversial crossbreeding was later sanctioned by Britain's Kennel Club, but the offspring had to be bred back to purebred Shih Tzu for three generations in England and six generations in the United States before they could be registered as purebred Shih Tzu. This delayed AKC recognition of the breed.

The Shih Tzu in America

The first Shih Tzu were imported into the United States from England in 1938. Because the AKC did not yet recognize Shih Tzu as a breed, the earliest imports were bred and shown as Lhasa Apsos. The earliest American descendents from the English imports tended to have heavier bones, broader heads, shorter necks, and denser coats than those dogs who descended from the early Scandinavian imports. The Swedish and Norwegian dogs tended to have longer, straighter legs, narrower heads, finer bones, and silkier coats.

In 1955, Shih Tzu were admitted by the AKC in the Miscellaneous Class, where they could not earn conformation championship points but they could compete for obedience titles. From this time on the breed rapidly gained in popularity.

What Is the AKC?

The American Kennel Club (AKC) is the oldest and largest pure-bred dog registry in the United States. Its main function is to record the pedigrees of dogs of the breeds it recognizes. While AKC registration papers are a guarantee that a dog is pure-bred, they are absolutely not a guarantee of the quality of the dog—as the AKC itself will tell you.

The AKC makes the rules for all of the canine sporting events it sanctions and approves judges for those events. It is also involved in various public education programs and legislative efforts regarding dog ownership. More recently, the AKC has helped establish a foundation to study canine health issues and a program to register microchip numbers for companion animal owners. The AKC has no individual members—its members are national and local breed clubs and clubs dedicated to various competitive sports.

The American Shih Tzu Club was formed in 1963 by the merger of the Texas Shih Tzu Society and the Shih Tzu Club of America. A third registry was maintained separately by a Mr. Curtis until full AKC breed recognition. The first Shih Tzu match show in the United States was organized by Swedish-born Ingrid Colwell, who did much to promote the popularity of the breed in the United States. Her mother, Ingrid Engstrom, was a well-known Scandinavian Shih Tzu breeder.

AKC Recognition

The Shih Tzu was admitted to registration in the American Kennel Club Stud Book on March 16, 1969. On September 1, 1969, the first day that Shih Tzu could compete for AKC championship points, the Reverend and Mrs. D. Allan Easton's Chumulari Ying-Ying won Best in Show at an East Coast show. That same day his sire, Jack and Mary Woods's Int. Ch. Bjorneholm's Pif, won the Toy Group at a show in the Midwest, and Pif's granddaughter Lakoya Princess Tanya Shu (owned by Jean Gadberry) won the Toy Group at a show in Oregon. Twelve days later, Pif became the breed's first American champion.

Initially, there was great variation in size and type among the Shih Tzu in American show rings. But over time, they became much more uniform. The current breed standard (discussed in chapter 1) was approved on May 1, 1989.

By 1969, some 3,000 Shih Tzu had been registered by the American Shih Tzu Club. By the early twenty-first century, the breed had become one of the top ten in the United States in AKC registrations, with about as many Shih Tzu now being registered with the AKC each month as were registered during the more than thirty years before AKC recognition.

Top Dogs

There are many well-known top producing and top winning Shih Tzu in America who have had a big influence on the breed. If you plan to one day show and breed dogs, knowing their names will be important as you peruse pedigrees and decide on a careful breeding program. If you just want a sweet pet Shih Tzu, it's still good to know who the top dogs are, because every purebred dog has a recorded pedigree and it's fun to look for the famous dogs among your dog's ancestors.

How can you recognize the top dogs? First, every champion dog has the letters Ch. in front of her name. On a top dog, you will also see the letters ROM after the dog's name, which stands for Register of Merit. The ROM title is

Outstanding dogs don't just do well in the show ring. They also produce great progeny.

Top Producers

In 1992, the members of the American Shih Tzu Club voted Ch. Lainee Sigmund Floyd, ROM, bred and owned by Elaine Meltzer, the most influential stud dog in the history of the breed. Ch. Tu Chu's Mezmerized, ROM, bred and owned by Kathy Kwait, was voted most influential brood bitch in 1993. They were considered to have had particularly significant impact on the creation of the more compact and elegant Shih Tzu seen in the show ring today.

Another legendary Shih Tzu is Ch. Lou Wan Rebel Rouser, ROM, bred and owned by Lou and Wanda Gec, who sired a record 130 American champions—more than any other Shih Tzu stud dog ever. Other influential stud dogs include Ch. Show Off's I've Got Rhythm, ROM (111), Ch. Lainee's Sigmund Floyd, ROM (69), and Ch. Dragonfire's Red Raider, ROM (52). Ch. Ista's Wicked Fantasy, ROM, Ch. Shente's Christian Dior, ROM, Ch. Paisley Ping Pong, ROM, Ch. Dragonwyck The Great Gatsby, ROM, Ch. Tu Chu's Munchkintown Art Deco, ROM, Ch. Hodari Lord of the Rings, ROM, Ch. Ming Dynasty's Devil's Play, ROM, and Ch. Shente's Brandy Alexander, ROM. Each has more than thirty champion offspring.

Ch. Gunning's Better Half, ROM, bred by Emily Gunning and owned by Dolly Wheeler and Emily Gunning, and Tammarie and Greg Larson's Akitzu Alwright With Ista, ROM, are tied for the top producing brood bitch with fourteen champion offspring each. Other top producing bitches include Charing Cross Cyd Charisse, ROM, Ch. Xeralane's Unlock The Magic, ROM, Ming Dynasty's Damme Alibi, ROM, Ch. Ali Aj Wildfire of R and R, ROM, Ch. Ming Dynasty's Chinese Sable, ROM, and Ch. Tu Chu's Mesmerized, ROM, each of which has produced more than ten champions—an unusually high number for this breed, because small dogs tend to have small litters.

awarded by the American Shih Tzu Club to dogs who have sired six or more American champions and bitches who have produced four or more American champions. Fewer than 600 Shih Tzu had been awarded ROM titles by 2005. While winning a ROM is based, in part, on the number of times an animal was bred and how many of the offspring were placed in show homes, ROM Shih Tzu have generally had a bigger-than-average genetic impact on the breed.

As of 2004, the all-time top winning Shih Tzu in the United States was Gilbert Kahn's Ch. Hallmark Jolei Raggedy Andy, ROM, bred by Diane Ehricht. Before his recent retirement, Andy surpassed the record of his sire, Ch. Charing Cross Rhinestone Cowboy, ROM, bred and owned by Gilbert Kahn and Barbara Finanger, by winning a record eighty-four all-breed Bests in Show and three national specialty shows (shows where just one breed is judged). For the names of some top ROM dogs, see the box on page 25.

Shih Tzu in Other Countries

There are records of Shih Tzu in Canada by 1935, where they were initially registered and shown as Lhasa Terriers. The first Shih Tzu registered under that name with the Canadian Kennel Club was English import Ah Sid of Lhakang, in 1952. Although Shih Tzu in Canada are registered in the Non-Sporting Group, as they are in Britain, there is very little difference between the Canadian and U.S. breed standards. Many Shih Tzu are shown and win in both countries.

European countries where Shih Tzu are popular include Britain, Ireland, Scandinavia, Germany, the Netherlands, France, Czechoslovakia, and Finland. Shih Tzu breeders are also active in Japan, the Philippines, Thailand, Australia, South Africa, Mexico, and many Latin American nations, as the popularity of this wonderful breed has spread throughout the world. Some Shih Tzu have also been recently reintroduced into China, although pet dogs are not legal in some parts of that country.

Chapter 3

What Do You Get With a Shih Tzu?

Shih Tzu get along well with strangers, children, and other dogs, and their small size makes them ideal for today's compact quarters. They are not yappy dogs. A Shih Tzu would probably bark if a burglar were picking the lock on your front door. Once the intruder was inside your home, however, your pet would be likely to give the intruder a guided tour! If you want a watchdog, a Shih Tzu is probably not for you. But if you want a small but sturdy, affectionate, and appealing companion to share your life, a Shih Tzu fits the bill.

Perhaps because of their long and intimate association with people, Shih Tzu seem almost human. Their faces can be very expressive. At times when a Shih Tzu is watching people talk, you would swear from his expressions that he understands what is being said. Many a squabble has been prevented by a Shih Tzu pawing in distress at the leg of a person who is raising their voice. Shih Tzu often enjoy watching television—and have definite likes about what they watch.

Hairy Fellows

Shih Tzu are among the few breeds that have hair (like humans) instead of fur. This means that many people who are allergic to fur are not allergic to Shih Tzu. It also means that Shih Tzu do not shed seasonally. Instead, they shed in small amounts all the time, just as you do. Much of this dead hair remains on the dog and causes tangling or matting. Because of the dog's profuse coat, the Shih Tzu requires daily grooming. If you are unwilling to either clip the dog down or devote the necessary time to care for his coat, you would be better off with another breed.

Temperament Differences

Because of their historical role as companion animals, you will find fewer sex-related temperament differences in Shih Tzu than in many larger breeds. Both males and females are loving and affectionate. Neither sex is aggressive, and Shih Tzu of the same or opposite sex get along well with one another. A male is easier to housebreak outdoors because he likes to mark his territory, but a female is easier to paper train if you prefer not to take your pet outside in the rain or snow. It is also easier to maintain a lush coat on a male, because hormonal changes associated with female heats can cause a female to seasonally lose some coat (called "blowing coat").

Temperament differences in this breed are related more to genetics than to sex. Some bloodlines tend to be softer in temperament than others. Softness is wonderful if you want an empathetic snuggle-bunny who will sense your moods and spend hours in your lap having his tummy rubbed. If you have small children or want a dog you can roughhouse with, however, a more outgoing Shih Tzu would probably be a better choice. This "tough-guy" temperament also tends to make a better show dog.

You can test your puppy's temperament to see if he is outgoing or soft. A dominant puppy will be very active and independent. A softer puppy will easily

While all Shih Tzu were bred to be sweet companions, each dog is an individual and will have his own unique personality.

accept handling and be much calmer and more reserved. In either case, the puppy should be curious and affectionate. And either type of temperament can be modified to some extent by the way a Shih Tzu is socialized as a young puppy (see chapter 5).

Self-Sufficient and Playful

Shih Tzu are very self-sufficient. If you are busy, they can and do amuse themselves for long periods of time, throwing and catching their own toys, racing around the house like furry dervishes, or curling up at your feet simply for the pleasure of being near you. Shih Tzu left alone during the day will usually sleep or play with their toys or perch at a window and watch the world go by. They are so easy to live with that many people with one Shih Tzu eventually get another. Breeders frequently joke that Shih Tzu are like potato chips—you can't have just one. Do remember, however, that the fact that Shih Tzu are not demanding dogs does not mean that they thrive in the absence of human companionship. They are definitely "people" dogs.

Even when your Shih Tzu is amusing himself, he will generally do so in ways that get your attention. Your dog might, for example, race back and forth from his toy box to the living room until every toy rests in a pile at your feet. When one of my Shih Tzu was determined to play catch while we were eating dinner, she batted a ball under the sideboard and began whimpering pathetically until one of us retrieved it for her. She'd learned that we always threw it (to keep her from putting it back under the sideboard). She got to chase the ball at least once, and if she was lucky we'd continue the game.

At a cocktail party a number of years ago, one of my Shih Tzu felt ignored. She lay on her back in the middle of the floor, nonchalantly juggling a toy with all four feet until she became the center of attention.

Most Shih Tzu are "toy freaks." One of my Shih Tzu's favorite toys

Your dog will not enjoy spending large amounts of time without you. Shih Tzu are "people" dogs, and love to be the center of attention.

is a large stuffed platypus. She "kills" this toy when she is frustrated, eats her treats on top of it, and sleeps using it as a pillow while holding her favorite yarn ball in her mouth.

Set Limits

Most Shih Tzu are chow hounds. The cabinet in my kitchen below the counter on which the dog treat jar rests needs refinishing after years of having Shih Tzu bounce off it during their enthusiastic acrobatics in response to "Do you want a cookie?" Every dog who ever visited my mother came back overweight because their soulful looks and tuneful yodels (tactics that don't work at home) convinced her that they were starving every time she ventured near the kitchen.

While three or four outings a day are sufficient for any Shih Tzu, my mother's canine guests got about six extra ones because she would take them out whenever they asked for a breath of fresh air.

Clearly, given an inch, your Shih Tzu will take a mile. This means you need to think about what you do and don't want your dog to do early on. Do you want to allow the dog on the furniture? Will he be allowed to sleep on your bed? Will he be confined (necessary for a puppy) when you are not at home? Clearly, he is not allowed to run out the front door when you open it or leave the backyard or chew the furniture or urinate on the Oriental rug!

Once you have determined the limits, be consistent. You will find that Shih Tzu are very anxious to please and that the combination of a single verbal correction when the dog is caught misbehaving and profuse praise for proper behavior are the best tactics.

Training Tactics

Sometimes being a bit sneaky is better than provoking a battle of wills, because a Shih Tzu can be stubborn. If your dog removes the *TV Guide* from the coffee table and chews on it every time you go for your morning walk—meaning you can never catch him in the act—why not just put the magazine someplace inaccessible for a few weeks until he forgets his fascination with that particular object?

Common sense is the real key here. If you get up the instant your Shih Tzu begins sneezing at you or washing your face at the crack of dawn, your pet will, of course, continue to do so. If he is teething on your antique furniture when you are away, why are you giving him this much freedom when there is no possibility that you will catch him in the act of misbehaving and be able to give him a timely correction?

The Dog's Senses

The dog's eyes are designed so that he can see well in relative darkness, has excellent peripheral vision, and is very good at tracking moving objects—all skills that are important to a carnivore. Dogs also have good depth perception. Those advantages come at a price, though: Dogs are nearsighted and are slow to change the focus of their vision. It's a myth that dogs are color-blind. However, while they can see some (but not all) colors, their eyes were designed to most clearly perceive subtle shades of gray—an advantage when they are hunting in low light.

Dogs have about six times fewer taste buds on their tongue than humans do. They can taste sweet, sour, bitter, and salty tastes, but with so few taste buds it's likely that their sense of taste is not very refined.

A dog's ears can swivel independently, like radar dishes, to pick up sounds and pinpoint their location. Dogs can locate a sound in $\%_{00}$ of a second and hear sound four times farther away than we can (which is why there is no reason to yell at your dog). They can also hear sounds at far higher pitches than we can.

In their first few days of life, puppies primarily use their sense of touch to navigate their world. Whiskers on the face, above the eyes, and below the jaws are sensitive enough to detect changes in airflow. Dogs also have touch-sensitive nerve endings all over their bodies, including on their paws.

Smell may be a dog's most remarkable sense. Dogs have about 220 million scent receptors in their nose, compared to about 5 million in humans, and a large part of the canine brain is devoted to interpreting scent. Not only can dogs smell scents that are very faint, but they can also accurately distinguish between those scents. In other words, when you smell a pot of spaghetti sauce cooking, your dog probably smells tomatoes and onions and garlic and oregano and whatever else is in the pot.

Tough techniques used by some obedience trainers to establish that you are the dominant "top dog" do not work well for most Shih Tzu. You are already much bigger than your Shih Tzu and are the source of the companionship and praise he craves. Shih Tzu perform obedience exercises well because they want to please you and because you have made it clear what behavior will elicit your praise or displeasure, not because they have been cowed into submission.

That Shih Tzu Charm

The unique charm that characterizes the Shih Tzu makes the dog a delight to live with—and also poses an obstacle to training. Training a Shih Tzu can be both an amusing and a frustrating experience. "Bad dog" generally elicits much tail wagging, many kisses, and lots of "Who, me?" looks of injured innocence. The general response when you try to discipline a Shih Tzu is, "How could you possibly be angry with me when I'm so charming?"

It's hard to remain stern with a Shih Tzu you have commanded "down" when the dog enthusiastically flips over onto his back and waves all four feet in the air, wags his entire body, and kisses the air. And how can you put up a topknot on a dog who is trying to kiss your nose while you are doing it?

You will find it impossible to be stern with your charming little dog for more than a few seconds. Enjoy the canine kisses, but also steel yourself to be a true leader for your Shih Tzu.

You have to steel yourself to avoid succumbing to that charm and letting your dog train you, rather than the other way around. Most breeders know of a home in which the situation escalated until the owners had a chubby, less-than-completely housetrained dog who roused them at five o'clock every morning or who kissed and charmed or pathetically whimpered his way out of being groomed so often that he got hopelessly tangled and had to have his coat shaved way down. Such behavior isn't fair to you or your dog, so be firm when necessary. Rest assured, your Shih Tzu will love you just as much if you teach him to be well behaved.

Chapter 4

Choosing Your Shih Tzu

O nce you have decided the Shih Tzu is the perfect breed for you, be sure you can offer a dog a good home for the rest of her life. This means taking full responsibility for her needs, investing the time and patience needed to make your pet a good companion, spending the money required to provide proper veterinary care, and making sure the dog gets enough attention, exercise, and grooming. These responsibilities are likely to last for ten to eighteen years, despite inevitable life changes such as new babies, moving, or returning to work. You may decide that this is not the time for you to get a dog, or that you would rather provide a home for an older Shih Tzu instead of training a young puppy.

Beginning Your Search

You should not take home the first adorable puppy you see. Resist impulse buying and bargain hunting. Raising sound, healthy puppies that are good representatives of the breed is not a money-making proposition, and there are no bargains on really good dogs.

Your puppy will be part of your family for many years, so it is important to make an educated choice. A knowledgeable breeder can help you choose a puppy who will suit your lifestyle—if you are honest about what you want and need in a dog, including your family activity level, experience with dogs, and knowledge of Shih Tzu. A very shy puppy will not do well in a noisy household with small children, just as a very dominant puppy won't flourish with a sedate senior citizen. If getting a Shih Tzu, any Shih Tzu, *right now* is your foremost concern, then you will get what you ask for—just any Shih Tzu.

Do not become fixated on a particular age, sex, color, or size. Shih Tzu puppies are slow to mature, and the American Shih Tzu Club recommends that they not leave for their new homes until they are 12 weeks old. Older puppies or adult Shih Tzu adjust readily to new homes. There are few sex-related temperament differences in Shih Tzu (see "Temperament Differences" in chapter 3). In fact, many knowledgeable breeders swear that males are more affectionate and easier to train to eliminate outdoors than females. All colors and markings are permissible in this breed, and a solid-color or dark-faced Shih Tzu does not have a problem with face staining. A Shih Tzu in the normal weight range (9 to 16 pounds) is solid and sturdy, as the breed should be, while Shih Tzu far below the norm may have health problems.

It is more important for you to ask about the temperament and health of the Shih Tzu you are considering than the sex, age, color, or size. How does her temperament compare to that of her littermates? Is she more or less active, dominant, cuddly? Because *all* Shih Tzu puppies are cute, try to see the puppy's dam, and perhaps her sire or other relatives, to give yourself a better idea of what she might be like as an adult.

Age, color, sex, and size are not as important as health and temperament when you are picking a puppy.

Be sure to ask if the required health tests have been performed on the puppy's parents (see chapter 8) and, where applicable, on the puppy herself. Do all the puppies seem healthy, with no mucousy discharge from the nose, no loose stools, and no foul smell from their ears? Are their coats clean and full? Do they have plenty of energy when awake? If you are going to try to keep your pet in a showy coat, rather than clip her down, you will want a strong, easier-to-care-for coat rather than a very soft, dense one.

If you feel intimidated or pressured to buy a puppy right away, keep looking. A responsible breeder is not interested in making a quick sale. He or she is concerned that the puppies go to suitable homes, and is willing to take them back if things do not work out.

Finding a Responsible Breeder

Responsible breeders are knowledgeable about Shih Tzu and try to breed dogs who conform as closely as possible to the breed standard. They represent their dogs honestly, and they know about and are working to control genetic conditions that may lurk in the background of the bloodlines, such as renal dysplasia, portal systemic shunt, hip and eye problems, allergies, von Willebrand's disease, thyroid disorders, and inguinal (groin area) hernias (for more on health problems see chapter 8). Their puppies have been properly socialized through gentle handling, human contact, and exposure to a wide variety of noises and experiences, to help them adapt easily to new homes.

Responsible breeders usually only breed when they have a waiting list of buyers and do not advertise in newspapers, put a sign in their yard, or sell their puppies in pet shops. They normally have only one or, at most, two breeds of dogs and only one litter at a time. They do not breed a female at every heat cycle or choose the sire without a lot of careful thought. They normally insist on selling pet puppies on mandatory spay/neuter contracts and/or limited registration (which means that if the dog is bred, the puppies cannot be registered with the AKC).

Some breeders will not sell a puppy to a family who has very young children. Others may make that decision after meeting your family and observing how the children behave around dogs and respond to directions about how to handle the puppies.

A responsible breeder starts the puppies off right with early socialization.

Champion Lines

Sometimes puppies will be advertised as coming from "champion lines." Is this a good thing? Absolutely! If a dog has many champions in her pedigree, it means she comes from a line of dogs who have been carefully bred to conform to the Shih Tzu standard—structurally sound, healthy dogs. When you look at her pedigree, you should see many dogs with the abbreviation "Ch." (which stands for champion) before their names. Not every dog in a pedigree will be a champion, and some very excellent producers have not been, but you should see several names with the Ch. title. If you see only one or two champions in the whole pedigree, or if the titles are back three or more generations, the term "champion lines" doesn't mean much.

When you take your puppy home, you should be given a three- to five-generation pedigree, a complete health record (documenting the necessary immunizations and a parasite check and treatment, if needed), and information to help you with feeding, grooming, training, and housetraining.

Your sales contract should give you at least two days to have your puppy checked by a veterinarian, and a written agreement to refund the purchase price or take the puppy back and replace it if it is found to be unfit by a veterinarian. An AKC registration form should also be provided and clearly explained.

The Adult Dog

Older Shih Tzu are very adaptable creatures and normally have no problems adjusting to a new home. The breeder may have an older puppy who did not turn out to be a show dog, or an adult who has retired from showing and/or breeding and would love to spend the rest of her life as a pampered pet. Such dogs may be already trained or be easier to train.

Dogs in breed rescue organizations who need loving homes may or may not have been responsibly bred. However, since they are adults, breed rescue organizations are able to evaluate them for any signs of a problem before you fall in love—something that can't be done with a puppy. They can also help you through the adjustment period. Remember that when you provide a loving new home to a dog who has been abandoned by her owner, you give her a new life!

What Your Veterinarian Should Know About Your Shih Tzu

No one can possibly be familiar with the physical and temperamental quirks of every breed, so here are some Shih Tzu peculiarities you might like to share with your veterinarian when he or she examines your new puppy.

Shih Tzu puppies often have slightly pinched nostrils that generally open with time. The bubbly discharge from a Shih Tzu puppy's nose is *not* serious if the discharge is clear and she is otherwise thriving. Even the nostrils of a dog who has difficulty simultaneously eating and breathing or is lethargic during the teething stage, when this problem is most acute, may open satisfactorily as the dog matures. A few dogs who are affected that severely, however, may require surgery later on.

Small umbilical hernias (a bubble-like protrusion of fat at the navel through an opening no larger than the tip of your little finger) are common in Shih Tzu and are often due to stress on the umbilical cord during delivery. Such hernias often close naturally over time, although you may want to have them surgically closed while your pet is being neutered.

Shih Tzu quite often cut their teeth relatively late and lose them relatively early. Undershot bites (when the lower jaw protrudes beyond the upper one) are characteristic of this breed, and crowded, poorly aligned, and missing incisors are common.

Reverse sneezing (a condition in which the dog seems unable to get her breath and begins to honk or snort) is quite common in Shih Tzu and is *not* life threatening. It is most often caused by a slightly elongated soft palate that "sticks" until the dog takes a deep breath through her mouth. The most effective way to stop this is to put a finger over your

Adult Shih Tzu can make great pets. They will love you as much as a puppy would, and won't make half the mess!

Shih Tzu's nostrils, thereby forcing her to breathe through her mouth. Sometimes just a hug and some reassurance will do the trick!

Part II

Caring for Your Shih Tzu

Chapter 5

Bringing Your Shih Tzu Home

Y ou should not bring your puppy home until he is *at least* 8 weeks old. Because this breed is slow to mature, the American Shih Tzu Club recommends waiting until a pup is 12 weeks old. This way your puppy has had an additional set of inoculations to protect against disease and plenty of time to be socialized with his mother and littermates and to begin to learn how to properly relate to humans and to the outside world.

This socialization process is particularly important if you have young children, who may not understand that rough play can frighten or injure a tiny puppy. (I always tell my grandchildren to sit on the floor to play with a puppy, so they won't accidentally drop or trip over the dog.) Everyone needs to become adept at sliding their feet along the ground in the "puppy shuffle," because Shih Tzu puppies are constantly underfoot!

If you have any questions at any time during your dog's life, don't hesitate to call the breeder. He or she has probably heard your questions many times before, but can't help you if you don't ask!

Preparing for Your Puppy

Before your puppy arrives, make sure you have everything he will need in his new home, and have created a secure and safe place where he can spend most of his time until he is housetrained and has learned some manners. Remember, he is still a baby and it is your job to safeguard him from harm! I prefer to paper train a puppy by setting aside a puppy-proof room, such as a laundry room or bathroom, with a baby gate across the door, so the dog can see out but can't get out. (See chapter 10 for advice on housetraining.)

Be sure there are no electrical cords, plants, hazardous household products, or other items your puppy might ingest or injure himself with—remember, all puppies love to put anything they can into their mouths. Provide your puppy with suitable toys for this purpose.

Puppies can and will get into everything, so it's your job to keep them safe by puppy proofing your home before your new dog arrives.

Food and Water Bowls

Your puppy will need a metal, weighted plastic, or ceramic food bowl heavy enough not to be tipped over and shallow enough for him to easily reach his food. His breeder will tell you the food your new companion is used to and may provide you with an initial supply; if not, purchase some of this same brand of food before you bring your puppy home. It is never a good idea to change food abruptly, because this can upset a puppy's stomach.

Fresh water should be readily available. Instead of a water bowl, many Shih Tzu owners prefer to use one of the large water bottles made for rabbits, which are available in pet supply stores. This keeps your puppy's face clean and dry and prevents him from taking a bath in his water dish. These bottles can be fastened to an exercise pen, screwed to a kitchen cabinet, or placed in a freestanding holder.

Leash and Collar

Your puppy will also need a nylon or leather leash and collar. Get a buckle collar, because a choke collar can easily get caught on something, and your puppy could strangle trying to escape if you are not present. A one-piece show lead with an adjustable neck opening works well for a small dog like a Shih Tzu. I do not like to let a Shih Tzu wear a collar indoors because it mats the coat. Some owners prefer to use a harness on adult Shih Tzu who tend to pull at the leash, because it reduces stress on the trachea.

Puppy-Proofing Your Home

You can prevent much of the destruction puppies can cause and keep your new dog safe by looking at your home and yard from a dog's point of view. Get down on all fours and look around. Do you see loose electrical wires, cords dangling from the blinds, or chewy shoes on the floor? Your pup will see them too!

In the kitchen:

- Put all knives and other utensils away in drawers.
- Get a trash can with a tight-fitting lid.
- Put all household cleaners in cupboards that close securely; consider using childproof latches on the cabinet doors.

In the bathroom:

- Keep all household cleaners, medicines, vitamins, shampoos, bath products, perfumes, makeup, nail polish remover, and other personal products in cupboards that close securely; consider using childproof latches on the cabinet doors.
- Get a trash can with a tight-fitting lid.
- Don't use toilet bowl cleaners that release chemicals into the bowl every time you flush.
- Keep the toilet bowl lid down.
- Throw away potpourri and any solid air fresheners.

In the bedroom:

- Securely put away all potentially dangerous items, including medicines and medicine containers, vitamins and supplements, perfumes, and makeup.
- Put all your jewelry, barrettes, and hairpins in secure boxes.
- Pick up all socks, shoes, and other chewables.

In the rest of the house:

- Tape up or cover electrical cords; consider childproof covers for unused outlets.
- Knot or tie up any dangling cords from curtains, blinds, and the telephone.

- Securely put away all potentially dangerous items, including medi-cines and medicine containers, vitamins and supplements, ciga-rettes, cigars, pipes and pipe tobacco, pens, pencils, felt-tip markers, craft and sewing supplies, and laundry products.
- Put all houseplants out of reach.
- Move breakable items off low tables and shelves.
- Pick up all chewable items, including television and electronics remote controls, cellphones, shoes, socks, slippers and sandals, food, dishes, cups and utensils, toys, books and magazines, and anything else that can be chewed on.

In the garage:

- Store all gardening supplies and pool chemicals out of reach of the dog.
- Store all antifreeze, oil, and other car fluids securely, and clean up any spills by hosing them down for at least ten minutes.
- Put all dangerous substances on high shelves or in cupboards that close securely; consider using childproof latches on the cabinet doors.
- Pick up and put away all tools.
- Sweep the floor for nails and other small, sharp items.

In the yard:

- Put the gardening tools away after each use.
- Make sure the kids put away their toys when they're finished playing.
- Keep the pool covered or otherwise restrict your pup's access to it when you're not there to supervise.
- Secure the cords on backyard lights and other appliances.
- Inspect your fence thoroughly. If there are any gaps or holes in the fence, fix them.
- Make sure you have no toxic plants in the garden.

Puppy Essentials

You'll need to go shopping *before* you bring your puppy home. There are many, many adorable and tempting items at pet supply stores, but these are the basics.

- **Food and water dishes.** Look for bowls that are wide and low or weighted in the bottom so they will be harder to tip over. Stainless steel bowls are a good choice because they are easy to clean (plastic never gets completely clean) and almost impossible to break. Avoid bowls that place the food and water side by side in one unit—it's too easy for your dog to get his water dirty that way.

- **Leash.** A lightweight nylon or leather leash will be easy on your hands.

- **Collar.** Start with a nylon buckle collar. For a perfect fit, you should be able to insert two fingers between the collar and your pup's neck. Your dog will need larger collars as he grows up.

- **Crate.** Choose a sturdy crate that is easy to clean and large enough for your puppy to stand up, turn around, and lie down in.

- **Nail cutters.** Get a good, sharp pair that are the appropriate size for the nails you will be cutting. Your dog's breeder or veterinarian can give you some guidance here.

- **Grooming tools.** Different kinds of dogs need different kinds of grooming tools. See chapter 7 for advice on what to buy.

- **Chew toys.** Dogs *must* chew, especially puppies. Make sure you get things that won't break or crumble off in little bits, which the dog can choke on. Very hard plastic or rubber bones are a good choice. Dogs love rawhide bones, too, but rawhide is not recommended for Shih Tzu; it softens and can get stuck in the dog's moustache or caught in the throat.

- **Toys.** Watch for sharp edges and unsafe items such as plastic eyes that can be swallowed. Many toys come with squeakers, which dogs can also tear out and swallow. All dogs will eventually destroy their toys; as each toy is torn apart, replace it with a new one.

Make sure your yard is as safe as your home. Shih Tzu puppies are tiny, and can slip through the smallest crack in a fence.

Make leash-training your puppy a game. Let him lead you initially, then gradually train him to follow you, using a food treat or a toy. If you have a fenced-in yard, get the puppy used to following you without a leash first.

Your Puppy's Crate and Bed

Young puppies need a lot of sleep. They tend to play very hard and then collapse in exhaustion. A small, enclosed crate (which is also approved for airline travel) with a towel in the bottom makes an ideal bed and den for your Shih Tzu puppy. It is small enough for him not to want to soil his sleeping quarters, yet easy to clean if he does have an accident. Later, you can use it when traveling with your pet. If you are using the crate as a bed in a puppy-proofed room or exercise pen, remove the crate door or fasten it open so your puppy is free to go in and out of his den as he pleases.

Once your puppy can sleep through the night without having to eliminate, you may want to have him sleep in his crate in the bedroom with the crate door closed. You want the crate to become a safe haven, not a place of punishment. You can initially encourage your puppy to enter the crate with treats and toys; you may even want to give him his meals there.

Do not get a dog bed made of wicker or wood, because your puppy could chew on it and harm himself. Many older Shih Tzu continue to sleep in their crates. Others like beanbag beds filled with Styrofoam pellets or hammock-type beds made of PVC piping and fabric. Any bed should have a washable cover. My dogs, I must confess, sleep on the bed once they are housetrained.

Limit Your Pup's Freedom

As soon as that first paw comes through the door of your home, Rufus (or Rufina) has to make many adjustments to become a part of your family. Your job is to help him fit in as painlessly as possible. An older dog may have some frame of reference from past experience, but to a young puppy, everything is brand new: people, furniture, stairs; when and where people eat, sleep, or watch television; his own place and everyone else's space; smells, sounds, outdoors—everything!

Puppies, and newly acquired dogs of any age, do not need what we think of as freedom. If you leave a new dog or puppy loose in the house, you will almost certainly return to chaotic destruction and the dog will forever after equate your homecoming with a time of punishment to be dreaded. It is unfair to give your dog what amounts to freedom to get into trouble. Instead, confine him to a crate for brief periods in your absence (up to three or four hours) and, for the long haul—a workday for example—confine him to one area he cannot destroy, with his own toys, water, and a radio left on low in another room.

At first, the entire floor of the puppy's special room (see chapter 10) should be covered with newspaper. To avoid inky feet, cover the newspapers with sheets of unprinted newsprint, available from a wholesale paper supplier or moving company. Your puppy will generally begin to eliminate in one corner of the room, away from the area where he sleeps and eats. Reduce the paper-covered area gradually to this corner. You may want to use urine-scented, plastic-lined puddle pads made for dogs (available in pet stores) or similar but less expensive unscented ones designed for use by incontinent people (sold in medical supply houses). These are ideal for paper-trained adult Shih Tzu.

To avoid wet feet and shredded papers, some people prefer to keep an unsupervised puppy in a large wire exercise pen with a Teflon-coated floor grate, with the crate inside the pen as a bed. Be sure to put paper under the pen to protect the floor in case the puppy has an accident. Some of these exercise pens have tops. If yours does, *be sure the top is securely fastened when the puppy is in the pen.* I know of one puppy who jumped up, managed to catch his head between the sides and top of a pen, and strangled.

When you limit your puppy's freedom, you make sure bad habits never develop.

For the first few days, when not confined, put Rufus on a long leash tied to your wrist or waist. This "umbilical cord" enables the dog to learn all about you from your body language and voice, and to learn by his own actions what objects and actions are met with "no!" and which ones are rewarded by "good dog." Housetraining will be easier with the pup always by your side. Speaking of which, accidents do happen. That goal of "completely housetrained" takes up to a year, or the length of time it takes a dog to mature. (For a complete house-training program, see chapter 10.)

To help your puppy sleep quietly at night, provide a night-light. You may also want to play a radio softly for the first few nights. Do not go to the puppy if he whines and barks when left alone because this will only encourage him to complain more vocally so that you will come back again!

Keeping to a Schedule

Until your puppy is totally paper trained or housetrained, adjust your schedule to his. He should spend the night in his room or pen and be put there when you go out or when you cannot keep an eye on him. The whole secret of successful training is to avoid giving your puppy a chance to have accidents on the rug or to chew on the furniture, thereby developing bad habits. Instead, praise him profusely when he uses the paper or eliminates outside or spends the night quietly in his room. By the time he is grown, he will need to be exercised only three times a day. These outings should take place on a regular schedule.

Some people prefer to keep even grown Shih Tzu paper trained. This is an advantage if you don't get home at the regular time one evening, if it is raining or snowing, or if your dog has an upset stomach when you are not at home to

Dogs like routine. Regular trips outside for potty breaks and play time will greatly speed your dog's training.

take him outside. If you adopt an older Shih Tzu who is not house-trained, you may, at first, want to use piddle pants or (for males) a belly band with a sanitary napkin when the dog is inside in the house. Be sure to remove it when you take the dog outside. After a few accidents in the house, the dog will decide to go outside rather than be wet and uncomfortable.

Socializing Your New Shih Tzu

Once your puppy has become accustomed to his new home and had his final puppy shots (usually given at 16 weeks of age), it is time to introduce him to the world. Many people take their puppies to puppy kindergarten classes or basic obedience classes, so the puppies can learn how to behave with other people and other dogs. If you have no children, your puppy can be introduced to youngsters by taking him to the playground or to a local mall. As he is introduced to new dogs and people and objects, be sure that your own attitude is confident, so your puppy knows there is no reason for him to be afraid.

When investigating new situations, your puppy should be praised and rewarded. Trying to force a puppy to approach something that makes him fearful or picking him up and fussing over him when he is nervous generally reinforces fearful behavior. Instead, gently encourage your puppy to investigate. (Food is a wonderful motivator.) If the puppy is still reluctant, try again another day.

The games you play with your new puppy at home will help him trust you and accept you as his leader, giving him confidence when he is in your presence and when he is exposed to new experiences. If you have adopted an adult Shih Tzu who is showing fearful behavior, the best thing to do is ignore him until curiosity brings him to you. Then reward him with praise or a treat, avoiding swift motions.

Praise your puppy when he comes to you when you call him; teach him to stand still when you touch him (very helpful when visiting the veterinarian); pick him up often; rub his tummy when he is on his back; encourage him to fetch and retrieve his toys and give them to you on command; teach him to allow you to take away his food or move him when he is sleeping; handle his

Lots of exposure to other dogs and other humans will make your pup a much better companion.

mouth, paws, and ears often. Most of all, be consistent, and use love and praise while teaching him that you and other members of the family are the leaders of his pack. Remember, too, that your puppy has a very brief attention span. Corrections are likely to have little impact unless you catch him in the act of misbehaving.

Chapter 6

Feeding Your Shih Tzu

Very young puppies are fed a special moist diet or soaked kibble until their first teeth come in. By the time you take your pet home, your Shih Tzu should be on a diet that is based on a top-quality dry puppy food. Puppies really do need specially formulated puppy food, because they are growing rapidly and need extra protein, vitamins, and minerals. Using dry food helps to prevent staining of the facial hair, because many canned foods are not only messy but also contain dyes.

Your puppy is your best guide to how much to feed. If she is regularly emptying her dish, you should feed her a bit more. If she always leaves food behind, you are probably feeding too much. Your puppy may go off her food when she is cutting her adult teeth, because her gums are sore and swollen. This is perfectly normal, and the dry food will help the teething process.

Understanding Dog Food Ingredients

Dogs have nutritional requirements that are different from ours and from other animals'. Pet food manufacturers select and carefully balance ingredients that provide dogs with the energy (from fats), protein, fiber (from carbohydrates), and vitamins and minerals they need, as well as considering taste and consistency.

Pet food manufacturers are regulated by the American Association of Feed Control Officials (AAFCO), which ensures that their products contain the appropriate amounts of nutrients, vitamins, and minerals. However, while most commercial dog foods meet AAFCO's minimum requirements, not all dog foods are created equal.

Reading Dog Food Labels

Dog food labels are not always easy to read, but if you know what to look for they can tell you a lot about what your dog is eating.

- The label should have a statement saying the dog food meets or exceeds the American Association of Feed Control Officials (AAFCO) nutritional guidelines. If the dog food doesn't meet AAFCO guidelines, it can't be considered complete and balanced, and can cause nutritional deficiencies.
- The guaranteed analysis lists the minimum percentages of crude protein and crude fat and the maximum percentages of crude fiber and water. AAFCO requires a minimum of 18 percent crude protein for adult dogs and 22 percent crude protein for puppies on a dry matter basis (that means with the water removed; canned foods should have more protein because they have more water). Dog food must also have a minimum of 5 percent crude fat for adults and 8 percent crude fat for puppies.
- The ingredients list the most common item in the food first, and so on until you get to the least common item, which is listed last.
- Look for a dog food that lists an animal protein source first, such as chicken or poultry meal, beef or beef byproducts, and that has other protein sources listed among the top five ingredients. That's because a food that lists chicken, wheat, wheat gluten, corn, and wheat fiber as the first five ingredients has more chicken than wheat, but may not have more chicken than all the grain products put together.
- Other ingredients may include a carbohydrate source, fat, vitamins and minerals, preservatives, fiber, and sometimes other additives purported to be healthy.
- Some grocery store brands may add artificial colors, sugar, and fillers—all of which should be avoided.

In general, with dog food you get what you pay for. That means the premium brands generally cost more but are also better food for your dog. You will find you can feed your dog less of a better food, and she will also be healthier, which may actually offset the extra costs in the long run. Quality foods are more completely used by the dog, as well, reducing the volume of stool. You can learn about how to read dog food labels and choose a good food for your dog in the box above.

Make sure you measure how much you feed your dog. Shih Tzu do not need unlimited food available all the time.

When and How Much to Feed

Young puppies should be fed at least four times a day with a food recommended by your pup's breeder. Many breeders simply leave dry food and fresh water available at all times for young puppies, or remove them only at night to prevent accidents.

As your puppy matures, you can cut down on the number of meals per day. By 6 months she should be eating just twice a day. You can change over gradually to an adult, small-size kibble when your puppy is a year old. The food should still be high in quality protein. Chicken, lamb, or some other protein source should be listed first on the package, rather than grain or rice.

In general, adult Shih Tzu eat about one cup of kibble per day. Again, if your dog is cleaning up her plate and is thin, increase her food. If she is leaving food behind or is getting fat, decrease the amount you are feeding. To keep your Shih Tzu from becoming a picky eater, leave your dog's meal down for only fifteen minutes or so by the time she is about 6 months of age. If she has not eaten, throw the food away and let her wait until the next mealtime. She will soon learn to eat promptly.

Obesity

Obesity is a common problem in mature dogs and can contribute to a variety of illnesses, including cardiovascular disease, pancreatitis, ruptured discs, diabetes, arthritis, and respiratory problems. Obese dogs are less able to regulate their body temperature and more likely to succumb to heat stress—a problem compounded in Shih Tzu by the profuse coat and short muzzle. You are not doing your dog a favor by overfeeding her!

If your dog has a distended abdomen or fat deposits along her spine and over the base of her tail, or if you can't easily feel her ribs through a thin layer of fat, she is probably overweight. Your veterinarian can tell you whether your pet should go on a diet.

Supplements and Table Scraps

If you choose to supplement your dog's diet, do so in moderation for a specific purpose. A teaspoonful of canned food, meat, cottage cheese, or cooked vegetables per meal to increase the dry food's palatability is sufficient. If your dog's coat is dry, you may wish to add a fatty acid supplement to her dinner. Many pets view heartworm pills and other supplements as treats. (Consult with your veterinarian before supplementing your dog's diet with vitamins.)

Feeding table scraps encourages begging at the table, contributes to obesity, and helps to create picky eaters. Dogs are perfectly happy with the same basic meal every day, unless you begin to feed them table scraps. At that point, they may hold out and refuse to eat unless you give them a favorite food, feed them by hand, or (and I have known several Shih Tzu like this) get down on the floor with them and coax them to eat off the floor! Why would you want to encourage your dog to behave this way?

Foods such as very fatty meats and highly spiced dishes are almost guaranteed to cause an upset stomach. A middle-aged or older dog who is fed rich table scraps and does not get enough exercise may develop pancreatitis. In mild cases, the dog may lose her appetite and periodically vomit or have diarrhea. In acute cases, her abdomen becomes rigid and extremely painful.

Other table foods are even more dangerous: Pork and chicken bones can splinter and puncture your dog's intestines; and chocolate, even in small quantities, is poisonous.

Feeding table scraps encourages begging, which is a very annoying behavior. It also contributes to obesity, which is as bad for dogs as it is for people.

Pet Food vs. People Food

Many of the foods we eat are excellent sources of nutrients—after all, we do just fine on them. But dogs, just like us, need the right combination of meat and other ingredients for a complete and balanced diet, and a bowl of meat doesn't provide that. In the wild, dogs eat the fur, skin, bones, and guts of their prey, and even the contents of the stomach.

This doesn't mean your dog can't eat what you eat. A little meat, dairy, bread, some fruits, or vegetables as a treat are great. Fresh foods have natural enzymes that processed foods don't have. Just remember, we're talking about the same food you eat, not the gristly, greasy leftovers you would normally toss in the trash. Stay away from sugar, too, and remember that chocolate is toxic to dogs.

If you want to share your food with your dog, be sure the total amount you give her each day doesn't make up more than 15 percent of her diet, and that the rest of what you feed her is a top-quality complete and balanced dog food. (More people food could upset the balance of nutrients in the commercial food.)

Can your dog eat an entirely homemade diet? Certainly, if you are willing to work at it. Any homemade diet will have to be carefully balanced, with all the right nutrients in just the right amounts. It requires a lot of research to make a proper home-made diet, but it can be done. It's best to work with a veterinary nutritionist.

Special Diets

In certain instances, a special diet may be called for. If your dog has diarrhea, your veterinarian may recommend that you give her Kaopectate and feed her cooked ground beef, rice, and cottage cheese to rest the intestinal tract until she returns to health. There are special kibbles that are lower in fat and calories for overweight dogs, and diets for smaller dogs, too.

If your dog has a particular medical problem, such as kidney stones, your veterinarian may recommend a prescription dog food designed for animals with such conditions. Two such special diets make the urine more alkaline or more acidic, and are used to prevent recurrences of different types of kidney or bladder stones. For a dog with food allergies, Solid Gold makes a cranberry-and-blueberry-based powdered supplement that can be used instead to make the urine more acidic. Unfortunately, a nonfood supplement to make the urine more alkaline is not yet available. Your pet's

It takes the best nutrition to keep a long, flowing coat in top condition.

stones must be analyzed by your veterinarian to determine which of these diets is appropriate.

Another type of special diet is low in protein for older dogs with kidney problems. While older dogs should not routinely be fed low-protein diets, kidney disease is common in seniors and, if they have it, a low-protein diet can help.

There are also special diets for dogs with diabetes and other conditions. Your veterinarian will prescribe them if your dog needs them.

If your dog seems to scratch excessively and does not have fleas, or frequently develops hot spots or the opportunistic yeast infections associated with allergies, you may want to switch to a kibble that uses a source of protein other than beef or chicken, and a grain other than wheat or corn. These ingredients, because they are in such widespread use, seem to provoke food allergies more frequently than other meats and grains. While many canine allergens are inhaled rather than ingested, such a switch may clear up your dog's itchy skin. Among the many alternate ingredients used in hypoallergenic dog foods are lamb, duck, fish, potato, and rice.

A water bottle can help keep your dog's facial hair clean and dry.

Dealing with allergies is often a process of trial and error, but be sure to keep your dog on the new food long enough to be sure it works (or doesn't) before switching to another product, and remember that any food change should be gradual to avoid stomach upset.

All-Important Water

We have already discussed the use of water bottles for your Shih Tzu in chapter 5. Whether or not you choose to use a bottle, fresh water should be available at all times. In general, a healthy, active puppy consumes about one ounce of water per pound of body weight. If your dog seems to be drinking excessive quantities of water, you may want to have your veterinarian test her kidney function (see chapter 8).

When traveling, it is a good idea to give your dog bottled water to drink because unfamiliar water can cause diarrhea. Some breeders add one capful of raw apple cider vinegar (available in a health food store) to one quart of bottled water to prevent tear staining on the dog's face. The vinegar changes the chemical composition of the tears. Water high in iron can also cause tear stains.

Chapter 7

Grooming Your Shih Tzu

Every time a novice owner looks at a beautiful Shih Tzu in the show ring with his coat brushing the ground, the first question is, "What do I have to do to get that gorgeous coat on my dog?" To a great extent, a profuse coat is inherited. Even more important, the coat is cared for carefully and regularly, and this care begins when you first bring your puppy home. You'll have to clean your puppy's face every day and cut his nails and trim the hair between the pads of his feet at least every two weeks, so he will have firm footing as his muscles develop.

The real key to a beautiful coat is regular brushing, so mats never have a chance to form, plus a bath at least once every three weeks. Because a dirty coat mats much more rapidly than a clean one, many show dogs are bathed every week.

Basic Grooming Supplies

Before you begin, you will need the following supplies, which can be obtained from your local pet supply store, a catalog, or online.

1. A pin brush with very flexible metal pins for basic grooming, and a soft slicker brush for touch-ups
2. A seven-and-one-half-inch comb (preferably Teflon-coated) with wide and narrow teeth placement for face and feet and to check for mats after brushing

3. A comb with rotating teeth or a rake with two rows of teeth set into a wooden handle in a V shape for removing large and stubborn mats (both of these tools also remove a lot of hair and are not recommended for show coats)

4. A pint-sized spray bottle (for water mixed with one teaspoon conditioner to mist the coat before brushing)

5. Latex bands and colored bows for topknots

6. Blunt-end scissors (for removing topknot bands and trimming sensitive areas)

7. Straight-bladed seven- to eight-inch stainless-steel grooming shears for trimming

8. A knitting needle or a comb with pointed end (for parts and topknots)

9. Human fingernail clippers (for small puppies) and canine guillotine nail clippers (for older dogs), and styptic powder (to stop bleeding if you cut a nail too short)

10. Ear powder and tweezers or ear hemostat (optional) for removing excess hair from inside the ear canal

11. A good-quality freestanding table or stand hair drier

12. High-quality shampoo and conditioner, plus tearless shampoo for the face

Basic Grooming Manners

Because Shih Tzu need a lot of coat care, you must get your new puppy used to being groomed regularly. It is best to begin by brushing your puppy in your lap every day, preferably when he is a bit tired and therefore likely to remain calm. Make grooming a loving time.

Your puppy may initially test you to see if he can convince you to stop. Some puppies shriek and squirm as if you were committing mayhem. *Do not give in,* but try not to make grooming a battle of the wills because some Shih Tzu can be just as stubborn as you are. It's best to use a firm "no!" when the puppy misbehaves, followed by lots of soothing and loving and kisses as you proceed.

If the puppy learns that good manners will be rewarded and that nothing he does will make you stop before you are ready, the tantrums (if any) will eventually cease. If you give in, things will only get worse, and you will wind up with a puppy who is impossible to groom and eventually becomes so matted that he will have to be shaved down. This is unpleasant for you and your dog, so persevere.

Brushing Techniques

As your dog grows more hair, you may want to do your brushing on a grooming table, especially after a bath. Because static electricity in a dry coat contributes to breakage, first dampen the coat slightly with the conditioner and water mix in your spray bottle. Brush gently and carefully in layers, beginning with the feet, legs, and belly, and working your way up to the center of the back. Brush in long, even strokes. Rotate the upper edge of the brush away from the dog at the end of each stroke rather than turning it inward and flipping the bottom edge of the brush up, which catches and breaks the ends of the coat. *Be sure to brush all the way down to the skin.*

If you encounter a mat, don't rip at it. Break it apart with your fingers before gently brushing out the dead hair. Large and stubborn mats will be easier to remove if you saturate them with conditioner and wait a few moments before breaking them up. In extreme cases, the rotating-toothed comb or rake can be used for dematting. Especially until you become used to the routine, go through the dog with the wide-toothed end of the comb when you are finished brushing to be sure you haven't missed any mats. Check especially in the armpits, on the legs, and behind the ears, where the most stubborn and easily missed mats form.

Once you have thoroughly brushed out your dog, use the knitting needle or parting comb to make a part down the center of the back and run the narrow-toothed end of your comb through the whiskers, holding the dog's head still by grasping his beard.

It is much safer to use a comb than a brush around the eyes. If your dog accumulates a lot of matter in the corners of his eyes, you may want to wash his face with a warm, soft cloth or wipe it with a damp cotton ball at this time. Then put up the topknot in a latex band, following the directions in the box on pages 62 and 63.

How often you will need to brush an adult dog will depend on the texture of his coat. Some Shih Tzu can be brushed only twice a week; others must be brushed every day.

Part the dog's hair and brush all the way down to the skin. It helps a lot if you have trained your dog to lie still on a table for grooming.

You can use a knitting needle to make a straight part down the center of your dog's back.

Many Shih Tzu "change coat" at some point between 8 and 12 months of age—that is, they lose their puppy undercoat and acquire their adult one. During this stage it may seem that the dog mats faster than you can brush, and this is the point at which many pet owners cut their dogs down. Don't despair—just keep on brushing. This stage is temporary and usually lasts for about three weeks. Believe it or not, if you've been careful and brushed out the dead hair religiously without badly damaging the outer coat, you will generally find your dog's adult coat easier to care for than his puppy one.

Topknots

A puppy topknot is generally placed fairly low on the forehead in a single band to catch all the short hairs. Do not pull the hair up too tightly into the band or the dog will rub at it.

Once your Shih Tzu has enough hair, it is best to put it up into a double topknot. This kind of topknot gives a more appealing expression, tends to stay in place better, and keeps the topknot hair from falling over into the eyes. You'll find step-by-step instructions for tying a double topknot on pages 62 and 63.

If you have many short and broken hairs on the head, you may want to rub in a drop of Bain de Terre Recovery Complex (a people product made by Zotos and available in beauty supply stores and some supermarkets) with your finger or brush in a little Shaw's Royal Coatalin (available from wholesale dog supply catalogs) to prevent further breakage. Human hair gel or Sticky Ticky (a canine product) can be used to "cement" loose ends into place when you want the dog to look especially attractive.

Grooming and Health Care

Every time you brush your dog, you have an opportunity to examine him closely for signs of a health problem. Watch for fleas or flea dirt (little black specks), check for ticks, and examine your dog's skin. If you notice any red or irritated spots (hot spots, caused by excessive scratching or chewing), medicate them immediately with antibiotic ointment.

Clean and check your dog's face every day, even if you do not brush him daily. If you see any signs of eye irritation, contact your veterinarian *immediately.* Neglected eye problems can quickly become very serious.

Check the anal area, too, to be sure it is not blocked by dried fecal matter. A puppy may have stool on the hair around the anus and then sit down, causing such an obstruction. If you see your puppy scooting his rear end along the floor or licking and biting at his rear, an obstruction is likely to be the cause— although this behavior can also be caused by fleas, tapeworms, or impacted anal glands. If the anal area is irritated, apply an antibiotic ointment.

Before bathing, check your dog's ears and remove excess hair from the inside of the ear canal by pulling it out with your fingers, tweezers, or an ear hemostat; ear powder will make it easier to grip the hair. Shih Tzu, like other breeds with dropped, hairy ears, are more likely to develop ear problems because the ear canal gets little air, making it a moist breeding ground for infection. Cleaning the excess hair out of the ear canal (not the ear flap, where the hairs have nerve endings that make extraction painful) improves air circulation and helps prevent infection. Some dogs never like having their ears cleaned! If yours is one of these, have someone help you hold your pet.

Bathing Your Dog

Try to make your puppy's first baths pleasurable experiences, so bathing, like grooming, becomes a normal part of his world. Be sure the water is neither too hot nor too cold (test it on your wrist), and try not to frighten him by soaking his face with water.

Never bathe a matted dog. Brush out the dog thoroughly first. Bathing sets in mats like cement, making them almost impossible to remove.

If at all possible, bathe your dog in a laundry tub with a faucet spray attachment. If you use the kitchen sink, you will have water all over the kitchen, and using a bathtub is very hard on the back. Be sure to place a rubber mat in the bottom of the tub to give the dog good footing, so he is less likely to struggle.

Ask your veterinarian to show you how to express the anal glands (when enlarged, they feel like two hard peas on either side of the anus just below the tail). Because the fluid these glands contain is extremely odorous, it should be expressed into a tissue while the dog is in the tub. Place your fingers on either side of the anus behind the glands and squeeze gently upward and outward to express the fluid.

Tying a Topknot

Part the hair between the eyes with your parting comb (photo 1).

Take the hair from the outside corners of the eyes (photo 2) and make a straight part just above the eyes across the middle of the foreskull (photo 3).

Put this, the first half of the topknot, into a latex band, then take a few hairs from the back of the banded section and pull them to anchor the back of the front topknot section tightly to the skull. This will "pouf" the front of the topknot, although you may want to

use the end of your comb to loosen the front hair even further.

Take a semicircle of hair behind the first section of the topknot and band it, again anchoring it to the skull (photo 4) by pulling up on a section of hair, this time in the front of the banded section.

Put a bow on the front section of the topknot, then band both sections together, placing this third band above the band on the front section and below the band on the back section. This will keep the hair in the finished topknot (photo 5) from falling forward.

A spray attachment in the sink will make it much easier to rinse your dog clean.

Once your dog is in the tub and thoroughly wet with warm water, shampoo twice. The first soaping removes the conditioner and surface dirt, and the second one gets the dog really clean. If you have hard water, any shampoo residue (which can cause itchiness) can be removed by pouring a quart of warm water mixed with a capful of cider vinegar over the dog, then rinsing thoroughly.

Bathe the head last, because this is what Shih Tzu seem to find least pleasant, and try not to get water in the eyes or into the ear canals. Do not use flea control products on the face.

After rinsing out the soap, put a capful or two of good conditioner into a quart of warm water and pour it over your dog, avoiding the face. Allow the conditioner to remain in the coat for a few minutes, then rinse. Leave some conditioner in the coat to reduce matting, rinsing only until the coat is barely slippery. You can experiment to see how much to rinse out on your own dog for best results.

Which Shampoos to Use?

Now we get to the much-discussed matter of shampoos and conditioners. No coat-care product is the magic answer for every Shih Tzu coat. Coats of different textures require different products, as do different climates and different tap waters.

If possible, ask your dog's breeder what products work best in his or her area for dogs with coats similar to your dog's. You will probably still have to experiment to see what works best on your particular dog. Unless a given product clearly isn't working, use it for a while. If you try something different every week, you will never know what works. Use recommendations from more experienced people as a guideline, not as gospel; we've all tried and discarded many recommended products before finding the right one for a particular dog.

Always use a tearless shampoo on the dog's face to avoid irritating the eyes.

Special whitener shampoos may help decrease the staining of white beards. If the staining is due to a bacterial infection, you can use an antibacterial shampoo that contains benzoyl peroxide (available from your veterinarian) to kill the bacteria. Be very careful not to get such products into the dog's eyes— a prebath drop of mineral oil in each eye will help to protect them. In very stubborn cases of infection deep in the hair follicles, your veterinarian may prescribe systemic antibiotics. Do not use bleach on the facial hair—it dries the beard and causes breakage and could easily injure your dog's eyes.

Postbath Procedures

Squeeze as much excess moisture as possible out of the coat. Then wrap your dog in a couple of thick bath towels and hold him in your lap for ten or fifteen minutes, using a corner of one of the towels to wipe his face and blot the ears. This procedure dramatically reduces the amount of time your dog spends under the hair dryer.

I do not recommend putting oil in the coats of pet Shih Tzu (a procedure used by some show dog owners to keep the hair from breaking) because the oil collects dirt and the coat tends to mat more when the oil is removed. Just leave extra conditioner in the coat after a bath to make brushing easier, particularly during the coat change described on page 60.

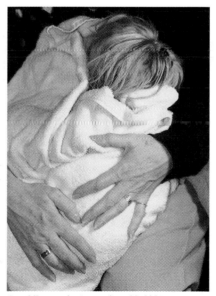

While your dog is swaddled in towels and more or less captive is a good time to cut toenails. The toenails are also softer and easier to cut when they are wet. Cut the nails to where they begin to hook over, being careful not to cut into the pink blood vessel (the quick) that can easily be seen if your dog has clear nails. If you do accidentally cut too deep and the nail bleeds, use styptic powder to stop the bleeding. Be sure to cut the nails on the dewclaws (the equivalent of your dog's thumb), if he has them. These nails do not touch the ground, so they will not wear down naturally like the others and can grow into the feet.

Swaddle your dog in towels and hold him in your lap for ten or fifteen minutes to reduce the amount of time he'll need to spend under the hairdryer.

Drying and Combing Out Your Dog

Thoroughly dry your dog with a blow dryer set on *warm—not hot,* which could burn the skin. Test the air from the dryer on your hand to make sure it is a comfortable temperature. Pay special attention to the hair under the ears and on the back of the neck, which take the longest to dry.

Brush the dog gently while his coat dries to separate and straighten the hair and speed the drying process. You will find it easiest to use a dryer that leaves both of your hands free to work on the dog—particularly if the dog in question is a squirming puppy.

Once the dog is dry, give your pet a part and put up the topknot. Now is the time to trim the hair between the pads of the feet level with the footpads, so it will not collect dirt, knot, and injure the tender skin. The hair on the top of the feet should be rounded, so the dog will not look like he has flippers, and the hair around the anus should be trimmed slightly for neatness. You may also want to trim the hair on the lower belly to keep it from becoming urine-stained and odorous, particularly on a male dog.

If your dog's coat is long enough, comb it down and trim it level with the tabletop all the way around while he is standing. This will remove split and uneven ends and make the coat look neater and fuller. Do not cut the hair on the muzzle short, even on a pet dog, because the short hairs will rub against the dog's eyes. This may cause injury and most certainly will increase the amount of discharge from the eye that probably tempted you to cut it in the first place.

Right after a bath is a good time to cut your dog's nails, because they are soft.

When you have finished, spray lightly with a little of your conditioner and water mix or a coat-finishing product to keep the hair in place. Then put your Shih Tzu down and watch your pet prance. He enjoys looking good!

Cutting Your Dog Down

I am notorious for preferring to have my dogs in long coats, although I have been known to cut off the topknots of dogs who look like unmade beds the minute they leave the grooming table. I trim the beard and mustache a little but leave them long enough to give me something to hold onto while grooming and to keep the mustache hair out of the dog's eyes. I cut the topknot hair about one inch long, slightly shorter above and between the eyes.

If you have neither the time nor the inclination to keep up a long coat, it is much better for both you and your dog to keep him in a cute clip than to have you feeling guilty and your dog badly matted, unattractive, and uncomfortable. You may want him trimmed short (one to two inches) overall in what is commonly called a puppy clip, leaving only the hair on the ears and tail and the mustache and beard long. Or you may prefer a more sophisticated trim that will make him look a bit like a Cocker Spaniel or a Schnauzer.

Trim the hair between the toes so that it is even with the bottom of the footpads .

You may want to have your dog trimmed by a groomer every six to eight weeks. If you choose to do the job yourself, you will need good electric dog clippers with #10 or #7 blades, scissors, and a slicker brush to keep pulling the hair out from the body while scissoring to achieve a smooth effect. When you clip or trim, be sure to begin with a clean, dry coat.

Not everyone wants to keep their dog in full coat all the time. A puppy clip is certainly a better choice than letting the coat get unkempt.

Choosing a Groomer

While you should always clean your dog's face and keep him mat-free, you may decide to have someone else do the really heavy-duty work of bathing, blow drying, nail clipping, ear and anal gland cleaning, and, if you wish, haircuts.

You might also have gone away on vacation or neglected your dog's coat-care regimen for some other reason and find the job of dematting daunting. Large mats *can* be removed with much time and patience. Try to avoid ripping mats out; the damaged ends will rub against other hairs, weakening them and causing further breakage. You might want to find someone experienced in dematting coated breeds to do the job for you, although this is likely to be expensive.

If you are looking for a regular groomer, the best way to find a good one is to ask neighbors, friends, your dog's breeder, or another Shih Tzu breeder in your area to recommend someone. Be sure your groomer enjoys working with animals and carries insurance for accidental injuries, and that the grooming area is neat and clean. Many reputable groomers belong to a professional association.

Once you've found a groomer that both you and your dog are happy with, be considerate. Schedule appointments well in advance and call if you will be late or need to cancel. Describe exactly what you want done to your pet to avoid unwelcome surprises.

Clipping down your dog's coat will not make him maintenance-free. He still needs regular brushing, plus vigilance against pests and skin problems.

How to Get Rid of a Tick

Although Frontline, K-9 Advantix, and BioSpot, the new generation of flea fighters, are partially effective in killing ticks once they are on your dog, they are not 100 percent effective and will not keep ticks from biting your dog in the first place. During tick season (which, depending on where you live, can be spring, summer, and/or fall), examine your dog every day for ticks. Pay particular attention to your dog's neck, behind the ears, the armpits, and the groin.

When you find a tick, use a pair of tweezers to grasp the tick as close as possible to the dog's skin and pull it out using firm, steady pressure. Check to make sure you get the whole tick (mouth parts left in your dog's skin can cause an infection), then dab the wound with a little hydrogen peroxide and some antibiotic ointment. Watch for signs of inflammation.

Ticks carry very serious diseases that are transmittable to humans, so dispose of the tick safely. *Never* crush it between your fingers. Don't flush it down the toilet either, because the tick will survive the trip and infect another animal. Instead, use the tweezers to place the tick in a tight-sealing jar or plastic dish with a little alcohol, put on the lid, and dispose of the container in an outdoor garbage can. Wash the tweezers thoroughly with hot water and alcohol.

Fleas and Ticks

These pests can cause great damage to your dog's skin and coat, so be sure to watch for the fleas themselves, excessive scratching, irritated skin, and flea dirt (black specks, which are flea excrement). If you see any indication of fleas, treat your dog with the products mentioned in the box on page 72. A severe flea infestation can cause anemia as well as hair loss, particularly in young puppies. In addition, some animals are very allergic to flea saliva.

Making Your Environment Flea Free

If there are fleas on your dog, there are fleas in your home, yard, and car, even if you can't see them. Take these steps to combat them.

In your home:

- Wash whatever is washable (the dog bed, sheets, blankets, pillow covers, slipcovers, curtains, etc.).
- Vacuum everything else in your home—furniture, floors, rugs, everything. Pay special attention to the folds and crevices in upholstery, cracks between floorboards, and the spaces between the floor and the baseboards. Flea larvae are sensitive to sunlight, so inside the house they prefer deep carpet, bedding, and cracks and crevices.
- When you're done, throw the vacuum cleaner bag away—in an outside garbage can.
- Use a nontoxic flea-killing powder, such as Flea Busters or Zodiac FleaTrol, to treat your carpets (but remember, it does not control fleas elsewhere in the house). The powder stays deep in the carpet and kills fleas (using a form of boric acid) for up to a year.
- If you have a particularly serious flea problem, consider using a fogger or long-lasting spray to kill any adult and larval fleas or having a professional exterminator treat your home.

To get rid of a flea infestation, you must treat the premises as well as the dog. Instructions on how to do this appear in the box above. Be sure to carefully follow the directions on the label of any product you use and to be very careful about combining products.

As you groom your dog, also keep a careful eye out for ticks. Instructions on how to remove a tick appear in the box on page 69. Ticks can transmit Lyme disease and other illnesses to your dog and to you, particularly if they are not removed promptly. If you live in an area where Lyme disease is endemic, you may want to have a licensed pest control operator spray the perimeter of your property. If your dog becomes lame after being bitten by a tick, he may have contracted Lyme disease. Contact your veterinarian about treatment, because Lyme disease, if left untreated, causes serious problems in both dogs and humans.

In your car:

- Take out the floor mats and hose them down with a strong stream of water, then hang them up to dry in the sun.
- Wash any towels, blankets, or other bedding you regularly keep in the car.
- Thoroughly vacuum the entire interior of your car, paying special attention to the seams between the bottom and back of the seats.
- When you're done, throw the vacuum cleaner bag away—in an outside garbage can.

In your yard:

- Flea larvae prefer shaded areas that have plenty of organic material and moisture, so rake the yard thoroughly and bag all the debris in tightly sealed bags.
- Spray your yard with an insecticide that has residual activity for at least thirty days. Insecticides that use a form of boric acid are nontoxic. Some newer products contain an insect growth regulator (such as fenoxycarb) and need to be applied only once or twice a year.
- For an especially difficult flea problem, consider having an exterminator treat your yard.
- Keep your yard free of piles of leaves, weeds, and other organic debris. Be especially careful in shady, moist areas, such as under bushes.

Other Itchies

Other causes of itching and skin problems in dogs include staph or other bacterial or fungal infections, various forms of mange (caused by mites), and allergies. Bacterial and fungal infections can be eliminated with special shampoos or medication prescribed by your veterinarian, who can also diagnose mites and provide insecticidal dips to eliminate them.

Allergies are often difficult to diagnose. If your dog's skin is irritated at only a certain time of the year, he may be allergic to a specific plant pollen. Your veterinarian may recommend a brief course of steroids to stop the cycle of itching in a dog with allergies, or perhaps a change in diet (see chapter 6), grooming products, or the environment. In severe cases, you may need to contact a specialist.

New Products in the Fight Against Fleas

At one time, battling fleas meant exposing your dog and yourself to toxic dips, sprays, powders, and collars. But today there are flea preventives that work very well and are safe for your dog, you, and the environment. The two most common types are insect growth regulators (IGRs), which stop the immature flea from developing or maturing, and adult flea killers. To deal with an active infestation, experts usually recommend a product that has both.

These next-generation flea fighters generally come in one of two forms:

- **Topical treatments or spot-ons.** These products are applied to the skin, usually between the shoulder blades. The product is absorbed through the skin into the dog's system. Among the most widely available spot-ons are Advantage (kills adult fleas and larvae), Revolution (kills adult fleas), Frontline Plus (kills adult fleas and larvae, plus an IGR), K-9 Advantix (kills adult fleas and larvae), and BioSpot (kills adult fleas and larvae, plus an IGR).
- **Systemic products.** This is a pill your dog swallows that transmits a chemical throughout the dog's bloodstream. When a flea bites the dog, it picks up this chemical, which then prevents the flea's eggs from developing. Among the most widely available systemic products are Program (kills larvae only, plus an IGR) and Capstar (kills adult fleas).

Make sure you read all the labels and apply the products exactly as recommended, and that you check to make sure they are safe for puppies.

If your dog's skin is dry and scaly, his coat is coarse and dull, and he has greasy skin, hyper-pigmentation, and a chronic offensive odor, he may have hypothyroidism, an inherited autoimmune disease occasionally found in Shih Tzu and many other breeds. Other signs of hypothyroidism include weight gain, neuromuscular and reproductive problems, and blood disorders. Your veterinarian can test for thyroid function and provide medication. A dog who has hypothyroidism must remain on thyroid medication for life. A thyroid panel and thyroid antibody tests should be done on any Shih Tzu who will be used for breeding.

Chapter 8

Keeping Your Shih Tzu Healthy

The Shih Tzu is basically a healthy dog with few inherited medical problems. *Many* of the health issues discussed in this chapter will probably never be a problem for you and your dog, but they will alert you to things you should watch for or tests you should have your veterinarian perform if you plan to breed your dog.

Finding the Right Veterinarian

When you bring your new puppy home, you will want to immediately take her to your veterinarian for a checkup. Most reputable breeders allow you a day or two to do this, and will refund your purchase price or replace your puppy if the dog is not healthy. A health and vaccination record should have been given to you when you purchased your puppy, indicating whether the dog has been tested for parasites, what inoculations she has had, what other shots she will require, and when.

It is important that you and your puppy establish a relationship with a veterinarian who is knowledgeable and caring. If you do not already have a veterinarian, ask your dog's breeder, other Shih Tzu owners, or other dog owners in your town for their recommendations. Choose your puppy's veterinarian as carefully as you would choose your own doctor. You must feel confident and comfortable with whomever you choose.

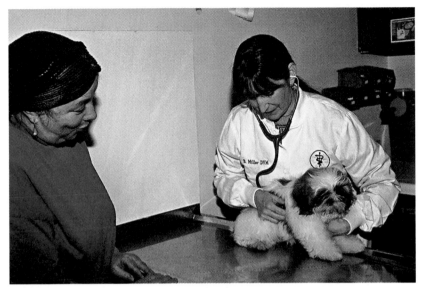

After you, your dog's veterinarian will be her best friend.

Because emergencies can happen on weekends or in the middle of the night, be sure the veterinarian you select is on call twenty-four hours a day or has ties to a twenty-four-hour emergency service.

While many specialized services are available only at large veterinary hospitals, you may prefer the more personalized atmosphere of a smaller veterinary clinic for routine care. Just be sure you find a vet who is willing to consult with specialists if an unfamiliar or difficult problem is encountered.

Today's high-tech veterinary care can be very expensive. Health insurance for pets is now available in most of the United States, although coverage is limited and most policies exclude older animals.

One of the best purchases you can make when you acquire your new puppy is a basic book on veterinary care, such as *Dog Owner's Home Veterinary Handbook* by James M. Giffin and Liisa D. Carlson. This practical guide can tell you what to do in an emergency and may help you identify signs of health problems in your dog, so you can discuss them knowledgeably with your veterinarian. A book, however, is not a substitute for veterinary consultation and care.

Routine Health Care

Many aspects of routine health care—such as checking for skin irritations and external parasites when you brush your dog, nail and foot care, ear and eye cleaning, and anal gland extraction—should be part of your regular grooming program and are discussed in chapter 7. During grooming sessions, you can also check for the presence of other problems, such as discharge from the genital region (indicating a possible infection and requiring veterinary attention).

Part of routine care is simply getting to know your dog: her normal behavior, her activity level, her appetite, and her elimination habits. Because you know your pet better than anyone else, you are likely to be the first to notice signs that she may be ill.

If she vomits or has diarrhea just once, you generally do not need to be concerned (unless you have recently been around a lot of unfamiliar canines). Dogs tend to eat anything and everything and promptly eliminate what doesn't go down well. If she continues this problem or repeatedly has mild bouts of vomiting or loose stool, particularly if she also appears lethargic, loses her appetite, or exhibits any other abnormal behavior, consult your veterinarian.

Do the same if your dog has explosive diarrhea and you have recently been around a lot of other dogs. The deadly Campylobacter bacteria, nicknamed

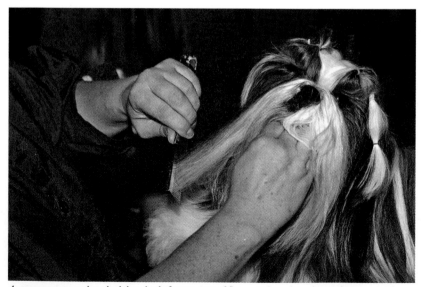

As you groom your dog, check her closely for any signs of fleas or ticks and any lumps, bumps, scratches, or sore spots.

As you get to know your dog, you will know when she is feeling under the weather.

"dog show crud," is highly contagious and often kills within twelve to twenty-four hours after the onset of symptoms, even with prompt veterinary attention. The box on pages 80–81 gives you more advice on when you need to contact your dog's veterinarian.

Taking Your Dog's Temperature and Pulse

If you suspect your pet is ill, you may want to take her temperature. Use a rectal thermometer coated with a lubricant such as petroleum jelly. Raise your dog's tail and gently insert the bulb of the thermometer one to two inches into her anal canal. Put one hand under her tummy to keep her standing and hold the thermometer in place for three minutes. A dog's normal temperature is about 100 to 102 degrees F.

Your dog's pulse, which is normally about 70 to 130 beats per minute at rest and faster in puppies, can be taken by gently pressing the femoral artery located along the inside of her thigh, where her back leg joins her body.

Giving Medicine

When you need to give your dog a pill, it's easiest to camouflage the medicine in liverwurst or peanut butter. (Just be sure to ask your vet first of it's okay to mix

Vaccines

What vaccines dogs need and how often they need them has been a subject of controversy for several years. Researchers, health care professionals, vaccine manufacturers, and dog owners do not always agree on which vaccines each dog needs or how often booster shots must be given.

In 2003, the American Animal Hospital Association released vaccination guidelines and recommendations that have helped dog owners and veterinarians sort through much of the controversy and conflicting information. The guidelines designate four vaccines as core, or essential, because of the serious nature of the diseases and their widespread distribution. These are canine distemper virus, canine parvovirus, canine adenovirus-2, and rabies. The general recommendations for their use (except rabies, for which you must follow local laws) are:

- Vaccinate puppies at 6–8 weeks, 9–11 weeks, and 12–14 weeks.
- Give a booster shot when the dog is 1 year old.

the particular medication with food.) If your dog still refuses to eat or spits out the medication, open her mouth, place the pill on the back of her tongue, gently hold her mouth closed, and stroke her throat until she swallows.

If you have to give your dog liquid medication, hold her head up by her chin whiskers and insert the medication in the pocket at the side of her mouth, letting it run through her back teeth and down her throat. If it's a large dose, give her a chance to swallow rather than pouring everything into her mouth at once.

Common Health Problems

Because it is impossible for a veterinarian to know everything about every breed, some of the breed-specific health quirks that affect the Shih Tzu are discussed in chapter 4. You may want to bring them to your veterinarian's attention.

- Give a subsequent booster shot every three years, unless there are risk factors that make it necessary to vaccinate more or less often.

Noncore vaccines should only be considered for those dogs who risk exposure to a particular disease because of geographic area, lifestyle, frequency of travel, or other issues. They include vaccines against distemper-measles virus, canine parainfluenza virus, leptospirosis, Bordetella bronchiseptica, and Borrelia burgdorferi (Lyme disease).

Vaccines that are not generally recommended because the disease poses little risk to dogs or is easily treatable, or the vaccine has not been proven to be effective, are those against Giardia, canine coronavirus, and canine adenovirus-1.

Often, combination injections are given to puppies, with one shot containing several core and noncore vaccines. Your veterinarian may be reluctant to use separate shots that do not include the noncore vaccines, because they must be specially ordered. If you are concerned about these noncore vaccines, talk to your vet.

Common Ear Problems

If your dog keeps shaking her head or scratching at or rubbing her ears, or if you notice a foul smelling or dark discharge when you clean her ears, consult your veterinarian. The problem could be ear mites or a bacterial or fungal infection, and the treatments for each are different. A neglected ear problem is painful for your dog and can become chronic, so do not wait to see if it goes away by itself.

Your veterinarian can determine the cause of the problem and provide appropriate medication. If you have to administer ear drops or ointment, your veterinarian will generally recommend that you clean the ear first with a special solution, wiping out the excess with a cotton ball. When giving ear medication, put it into the ear and then massage the base of the ear to be sure the medication gets down into the ear canal. Never poke deep into the ear canal with a swab or other pointed object. This can cause serious injury. Clean only what you can see.

When to Call the Veterinarian

Go to the vet right away or take your dog to an emergency veterinary clinic if:

- Your dog is choking
- Your dog is having trouble breathing
- Your dog has been injured and you cannot stop the bleeding within a few minutes
- Your dog has been stung or bitten by an insect and the site is swelling
- Your dog has been bitten by a snake
- Your dog has been bitten by another animal (including a dog) and shows any swelling or bleeding
- Your dog has touched, licked, or in any way been exposed to a poison
- Your dog has been burned by either heat or caustic chemicals
- Your dog has been hit by a car
- Your dog has any obvious broken bones or cannot put any weight on one of her limbs
- Your dog has a seizure

Make an appointment to see the vet as soon as possible if:

- Your dog has been bitten by a cat, another dog, or a wild animal
- Your dog has been injured and is still limping an hour later
- Your dog has unexplained swelling or redness

Common Eye Problems

Because Shih Tzu have large eyes set in shallow sockets, their eyes may be especially prone to injury. If your dog's eyes are red or cloudy or tear excessively, or if she keeps squinting and rubbing at her eye, get her to your veterinarian *immediately.* If she has an eye injury or is developing an infection, prompt treatment can prevent scarring or possibly even the loss of an eye.

When grooming your dog, be careful not to pull back on the hair on the head and forehead until the eyes bulge. Short-faced dogs with shallow eye sockets such as the Shih Tzu are also more prone to traumatic proptosis, in which the eye is dislodged from the socket. The eyelids then close behind the eye, cutting off the supply of oxygen to the eye. Proptosis can cause blindness and loss of the eye if not treated by a veterinarian within twenty minutes.

- Your dog's appetite changes
- Your dog vomits repeatedly and can't seem to keep food down, or drools excessively while eating
- You see any changes in your dog's urination or defecation (pain during elimination, change in regular habits, blood in urine or stool, diarrhea, foul-smelling stool)
- Your dog scoots her rear end on the floor
- Your dog's energy level, attitude, or behavior changes for no apparent reason
- Your dog has crusty or cloudy eyes, or excessive tearing or discharge
- Your dog's nose is dry or chapped, hot, crusty, or runny
- Your dog's ears smell foul, have a dark discharge, or seem excessively waxy
- Your dog's gums are inflamed or bleeding, her teeth look brown, or her breath is foul
- Your dog's skin is red, flaky, itchy, or inflamed, or she keeps chewing at certain spots
- Your dog's coat is dull, dry, brittle, or bare in spots
- Your dog's paws are red, swollen, tender, or cracked, or the nails are split or too long
- Your dog is panting excessively, wheezing, unable to catch her breath, breathing heavily, or sounds strange when she breathes

Among the hereditary eye problems found in Shih Tzu are juvenile cataracts and progressive retinal atrophy (PRA), both of which lead to blindness. Both diseases are relatively rare in the breed, and a dog with either condition should never be bred.

Corneal ulcers are the most serious eye problem commonly affecting Shih Tzu. An ulcer looks like a small dot on the dark part of the eye. The pupil may appear bluish, and the white of the eye is usually red and inflamed.

A corneal ulcer can be caused by irritation, such as from abnormally placed eyelashes, or by injury (be careful using the comb and brush around your dog's eyes). It may also occur spontaneously. If the dog is unable to properly close her eyelid over the cornea, or suffers from dry eye (an abnormality of the tear film), it can cause chronic corneal ulceration and may require daily eye drops for the life of your dog.

Regularly check your dog's eyes for foreign matter, discharge, debris, or injury.

If your dog has or is developing a corneal ulcer, prompt treatment is essential. An untreated ulcer can cause the cornea to rupture. See your veterinarian at once. Your dog should be given a drop of atropine in the affected eye twice daily, coupled with a drop of Betadyne, which aids in healing, and an antibiotic that does not contain steroids. Your veterinarian will probably instruct you to administer the antibiotic three or four times a day, but every two hours is better if you can.

When administering eye drops, pull out the lower lid to make a pocket, and drop the medication into this pocket. If the dog continues to rub at her eye, you may need to use a cone-shaped device called an Elizabethan collar, or the newer (and more comfortable) bite-not collar, both of which prevent a dog from reaching her body with her mouth or her face with her feet, thus avoiding further injury. Once the ulcer has healed, your vet will probably want you to follow up with an antibiotic containing steroids to reduce or eliminate scarring.

Common Problems With the Teeth and Gums

The Shih Tzu's undershot bite frequently causes her to lose some of her front teeth at an early age. Missing or misaligned teeth and retained baby teeth are also quite common in the breed.

Your Shih Tzu will begin to acquire her permanent teeth at about 4 or 5 months of age. At this time her gums may become swollen and sore, and she may go off her food. Dog biscuits and hard chew toys help the permanent teeth emerge. If you notice a retained baby tooth, wiggle it with your fingernail to help it come out. Retained baby teeth can cause the permanent teeth to be pushed out of alignment.

To prevent tooth decay and gum disease, give your dog kibble, dog biscuits, and hard toys to chew on, and have your veterinarian show you how to clean your dog's teeth. If tartar and plaque build up, you may have to have your veterinarian professionally clean your dog's teeth, so it is best to make dental care part of your regular routine. Neglected teeth and gums can lead to infection and can cause serious health problems for your dog.

Problems Associated With a Short Face

The short face of the Shih Tzu can contribute to various health problems because the nasal cavity, pharynx, larynx, and surrounding tissues are compressed into a small space.

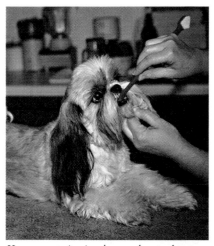

Have your veterinarian show you how to clean your dog's teeth. An ounce of prevention now will head off pounds of dental trouble.

All short-faced breeds are more prone to heat exhaustion and must be exercised modestly and watched carefully in hot weather.

Shih Tzu puppies may snore, snort, bubble, or sniffle, particularly while teething. These symptoms normally correct themselves as the dog matures, and are no cause for concern if the nasal discharge is clear and the dog is thriving. If your dog's nostrils are extremely pinched even after she has cut her adult teeth, you may wish to have her examined by a specialist.

Severe snorting respiration and difficulty in breathing may, in rare cases, lead to cyanosis and collapse due to obstructive respiratory disease caused by stenotic nares (collapsed nostrils), elongated soft palate, and other structural problems. In such extreme cases, corrective surgery may be necessary to open the airway. Some veterinarians unfamiliar with the breed are much too quick to recommend such surgery, though. If your dog is thriving or still cutting her teeth, give things a little time.

All short-faced breeds are especially vulnerable to heatstroke and breathing problems, so exercise with caution in the warmer months.

Internal Parasites

Internal parasites can plague even the most well-cared-for dogs in the cleanest of homes. And in small breeds, infestations tend to be more serious—especially in young puppies. Take a stool sample to your veterinarian when you take your puppy for her annual checkup and heartworm test, or if any signs cause you to suspect that parasites are present.

If you do see signs of parasites, it is best to let your vet diagnose the problem and prescribe specific medication for that specific parasite. Over-the-counter deworming medications do not work for all types of parasites, and so may not be right for your dog's situation.

Tapeworms

Tapeworms can be detected by finding tapeworm segments around the anus or in the stool. Fresh segments are white and may move; dried ones look like grains of brown rice. Tapeworms can be acquired from uncooked meat or fish but are most commonly transmitted by fleas, which serve as an intermediate host after eating tapeworm eggs.

If your dog has tapeworms, she may have diarrhea, dry itchy skin, or weight loss. She may bite at her rear when a tapeworm segment is emerging. Your veterinarian can provide you with appropriate medication, but the infestation is likely to recur unless the flea hosts are eliminated as well (see "New Products in the Fight Against Fleas" in chapter 7).

Roundworms

Dogs contract roundworms through contact with soil containing the eggs. They look like strands of spaghetti, and can be seen in the stool or may be vomited. Many puppies are born with roundworms because the parasites can encyst in the tissue of the mother and remain dormant until the late stages of pregnancy, when they can be passed along to her puppies.

Roundworms are not very serious in adult dogs (they must still be treated, though), but they can make a young puppy severely ill. A puppy with roundworms may have a potbelly and a dull coat. She may vomit or have diarrhea and fail to gain weight. Your veterinarian can check for the parasite in your puppy's stool and provide medication to kill the worms. Generally, the dog must be wormed twice to eliminate immature roundworms that are not killed by the first dose.

Hookworms

Hookworms are small and thin. They fasten themselves to the wall of the small intestine and draw blood from their host. The most common signs of hookworm are anemia, blood in the stool, and diarrhea. The eggs can be picked up from contaminated soil or feces, or passed to a puppy by her mother.

Your veterinarian can confirm that your puppy has hookworms by the presence of eggs in the stool, and provide an appropriate worming preparation.

Whipworms

Whipworms are threadlike worms that are thicker at one end; they are acquired from contaminated soil. Whipworms may cause diarrhea and weight loss. They are difficult to detect, and it may require several fecal examinations for your veterinarian to identify them and prescribe an appropriate treatment. Follow up with several fecal checks to be sure the worms have been eliminated.

The same is true for threadworms, which cause watery diarrhea and signs of lung infection.

Internal parasites will rob your dog of nutrition and make it impossible to keep up that gorgeous coat.

Heartworms

Heartworms, which are transmitted by infected mosquitoes, are a serious problem in much of the United States. Adult worms inhabit the lungs and heart of their host, and may eventually cause death. An affected dog generally has a soft, deep cough that is exacerbated by exercise. She may appear weak and lose weight. Your veterinarian can confirm the presence of heartworms by finding larvae (called microfilaria) in your dog's blood.

Before beginning preventive heartworm medication, your dog must have a blood test to be sure she does not have heartworm. Only a young puppy who has never been exposed to mosquitoes does not need a blood test first. If your dog has heartworm, giving her the preventive medication could kill her.

Treatment is difficult and dangerous, while prevention is easy and safe. So if you live in or plan to visit an area where heartworm is found, your dog should be on preventive medication. In warm areas, your dog will probably always be on a preventive. In colder areas where mosquitoes die out in winter, preventive medication may be needed only from spring until the start of winter. Your veterinarian will know what's best.

I prefer to give heartworm preventive medication in monthly doses, because some researchers have linked the longer-lasting form to various autoimmune disorders. If you fear you will forget to give the monthly medication, however, use the longer-acting one.

Protozoans

Several common canine ailments, including coccidiosis, trichomoniasis, and giardiasis, are caused by one-celled animals called protozoans. These diseases are usually caused by a dog drinking contaminated water—a puddle in the street, a stream in the park, or poor sanitation. All can lead to severe diarrhea. Toxoplasmosis, which can be passed to humans, can affect the brain, lungs, and lymph system. It is detected by blood tests. Piroplasmosis, or canine babesiosis, is a serious protozoan disease that destroys red blood cells. It is transmitted by the brown dog tick and can be detected and treated by your veterinarian.

Inherited Disorders

A number of inherited disorders can be found in Shih Tzu, in addition to the hypothyroidism and eye problems discussed earlier. When a disease lurks in a breed's gene pool, this does not mean every dog has the disease or even carries the gene for the disease. It does mean the disease is more likely to occur in the

Problems that lurk in a breed's gene pool will not show up in every dog. But you must ask the dog's breeder what they are doing to minimize them.

breed. That's why it's important to ask the breeder you are considering buying a puppy from about what they are doing to minimize these problems in their dogs' bloodlines. It's also important to recognize the signs of these diseases, so you can get prompt veterinary care for your Shih Tzu.

Auto-Immune Disorders

Shih Tzu, like many breeds of dogs, are affected by several auto-immune disorders. Hypothyroidism is perhaps the most common; it occurs when the thyroid fails to produce sufficient hormones. The resulting deficiency causes hair to become brittle and fall out easily. The dog's skin will also get thick and turn a darker color. Thyroid hormones control metabolism, so a dog with hypothyroidism will be lethargic, tend to be fat, and will have limited energy. The deficiency can range from mild to severe; mild cases may not even show signs, although a blood test can detect the problem.

Another immune disorder is von Willebrand's disease (vWD), a blood clotting disorder. Testing for vWD is strongly recommended, because a dog with severe vWD disease could bleed to death during routine surgery. Your veterinarian can draw the blood for this test, but it must be drawn and shipped in a very specific manner. In the absence of such a test, have your vet do a toenail bleeding test before surgery to be sure your dog's blood is clotting normally.

Other disorders of the immune system include various forms of blood cancer and autoimmune hemolytic anemia, in which the dog's immune system destroys her own red blood cells.

Bone and Joint Disorders

Like other breeds, Shih Tzu may inherit hip dysplasia and other bone and joint disorders such as spinal disk problems, slipping kneecaps, popping hocks, and elbow dysplasia. Although such disorders in small breeds generally tend not to be crippling, they can be very painful. There are a variety of treatment options to minimize your dog's pain and maximize functioning.

If you plan to have your dog jump in obedience or agility, first have her hips and elbows checked by the Orthopedic Foundation for Animals or PennHIP for soundness.

Lameness in elderly dogs may be caused by arthritis. Your veterinarian may recommend baby aspirin to relieve the pain of arthritis and moderate exercise to prevent joint stiffness. Glucosamine, a neutraceutical, has also proven effective for some dogs with arthritis.

Heart Disease

Heart disease can be either inherited or acquired. When your dog visits your veterinarian for her annual physical, her heart will be checked for signs of abnormality. Some of the symptoms of heart disease include labored breathing, coughing or wheezing, weakness, loss of appetite, and a watery swelling of the abdomen (edema). Surgery or therapy can repair or improve some cardiac problems, or greatly extend the life of an affected pet.

Hernias

Small umbilical hernias are frequently found in Shih Tzu puppies. These may be the result of an inherited weakness or may be due to tension on the umbilical cord at birth. Unless they are very large, these hernias usually close by themselves. Inguinal hernias, found in the groin area, are much more serious. Many will require surgical correction, and dogs with inguinal hernias should not be bred.

Juvenile Renal Dysplasia

This developmental defect of the kidneys is the most serious inherited disorder found in Shih Tzu. It is also present in Lhasa Apsos and, less frequently, in some other breeds. In a dog with juvenile renal dysplasia (JRD), the glomeruli (the filtering structure of the kidneys, where toxins, fluid, and electrolytes are removed from the blood) fail to develop properly. In severe cases, JRD causes death at an early age.

Severely affected puppies drink and urinate excessively and are smaller than normal (generally less than three pounds at 5 months of age). Rather quickly they begin to vomit, become weak, debilitated, and dehydrated, and ultimately die of kidney failure.

Only a small percentage of Shih Tzu are severely affected by JRD and will die of renal failure. Most moderately and slightly affected puppies will live normal life spans with apparently normal renal function, while silently passing JRD to their offspring.

The presence of JRD should be suspected in puppies with elevated BUN and creatinine levels in their blood and extremely dilute urine as measured by a urine-specific gravity test, but these tests remain normal until more than 70 percent of the kidney is destroyed. They may also be abnormal due to the presence of other kidney problems, so they are of no value in detecting moderately and slightly affected dogs.

Currently, the only definitive test for JRD is a wide wedge kidney biopsy. It is unwise to biopsy animals with poor results on blood and urine tests because they are a surgical risk. An ultrasound examination of the kidneys may detect moderate carriers, and some breeders are using a linked marker genetic test to reduce the frequency of JRD in their litters.

Signs such as those just described in an elderly dog may be a sign of various "old age" kidney diseases found in all breeds of dogs. Again, your veterinarian will want to perform blood and urine tests and perhaps prescribe a special diet. These diseases can also obscure the presence of renal dysplasia in the tissue of elderly animals.

> **TIP**
>
> **JRD Research**
>
> To gain more knowledge about JRD and, hopefully, develop a definitive noninvasive genetic test, the American Shih Tzu Club Charitable Trust (www.shihtzu.org) is funding JRD research. If you can provide tissue or cheek swab samples from an affected dog or would like to contribute to JRD research, contact JoAnn Gustafson (ningsia@nwlink.com) or Jo Ann White (joawhite@juno.com).

If you choose a dog from a breeder who understands genetics and works hard to breed healthy dogs, your Shih Tzu companion should be with you for a long time.

Portosystemic Shunt

This inherited disorder may be found, in rare instances, in Shih Tzu and several other small breeds. In a dog with a portosystemic shunt, blood is diverted around the liver into the bloodstream without being detoxified. Many cases are diagnosed in young animals. Those affected are depressed, thin, and have trouble gaining weight. They may periodically exhibit peculiar behavior, such as bouts of aggression, staggering, pacing, circling, head pressing, blindness, deafness, tremors, and seizures.

Your veterinarian can test for the presence of this disorder and provide a special diet. The defect can be surgically corrected; without surgery, severely affected animals probably will die of liver failure.

Stones

Shih Tzu may develop kidney or bladder stones. Symptoms of stones include urinary blockage, painful voiding, blood in the urine, and cystitis. Large stones are generally removed surgically. Smaller stones can be dissolved and new stones prevented from forming with a special diet prescribed by your veterinarian. Infections and other types of obstructions may cause similar signs, all of which should be treated promptly by your veterinarian.

Poisoning

Among the most common household products that can poison dogs are antifreeze (ethylene glycol), rat poison (anticoagulants such as wafarin and brodifacoum), matches, and human drugs (including acetaminophen, aspirin, boric acid, phenol, sleeping pills, and laxatives). Other ingredients in your bathroom that could poison your dog include deodorants, hair colorings, nail polish and nail polish remover, permanent wave lotion, rubbing alcohol, soaps, and suntan lotion.

Do not let your dog explore the kitchen cabinets—she could poison herself with bleach, cleaning fluid, deodorizers, detergent, disinfectant, drain cleaner, dye, furniture and metal polish, lye, mothballs, or shoe polish. In your garage, she might find brake fluid, carburetor cleaner, fungicides, herbicides, insecticides, gasoline, kerosene, lead, mineral spirits, paint, photographic developer, tar, turpentine, windshield washer fluid, or wood preservative.

A number of houseplants, including avocado, dieffenbachia, English ivy, jasmine, philodendron, and the bulbs of the amaryllis, daffodil, hyacinth, narcissus, iris, and tulip are poisonous. So are apple seeds, cherry pits, chocolate,

ASPCA Animal Poison Control Center

The ASPCA Animal Poison Control Center has a staff of licensed veterinarians and board-certified toxicologists available 24 hours a day, 365 days a year. The number to call is (888) 426-4435. You will be charged a consultation fee of $50 per case, charged to most major credit cards. There is no charge for follow-up calls in critical cases. At your request, they will also contact your veterinarian. Specific treatment and information can be provided via fax. Put the number in large, legible print with your other emergency telephone numbers. Be prepared to give your name, address, and phone number; what your puppy has gotten into (the amount and how long ago); your puppy's breed, age, sex, and weight; and what signs and symptoms the puppy is showing. You can log onto www.aspca.org and click on "Animal Poison Control Center" for more information, including a list of toxic and nontoxic plants.

mushrooms, peaches, rhubarb, tobacco, and walnuts. At Christmas, be sure your dog does not ingest holly or mistletoe berries. Whatever marijuana and jimson weed may do to your own health, they are definitely toxic to your dog!

When your dog is outside in your yard, do not let her eat andromeda, arrow-grass, azalea, bittersweet, boxwood, buttercups, caladium, castor beans, choke-cherry, climbing lily, crown of thorns, daphne, delphinium, dieffenbachia, dumb cane, elderberry, elephant ear, foxglove, hemlock, hydrangea, laburnum, larkspur, laurel, locoweed, marigold, monkshood, nightshade, oleander, poison ivy, privet, rhododendron, snow on the mountain, stinging nettle, toadstools, wisteria, or yew.

These lists cover the most common causes of poisoning in dogs, but they are by no means complete!

To treat poisoning, it is important to know what your dog has ingested. If you have any questions, call the poison control hotline listed in the box on page 91.

In general, you should try to induce vomiting unless your dog has swallowed an acid, alkali, solvent, heavy-duty cleanser, rodent poison, or a petroleum product, any of which would severely damage the esophagus if vomited. Also do not induce vomiting if your dog has swallowed sharp objects or tranquilizers, if she is very depressed or comatose, or if the poison has been in the dog's system for more than two hours.

Your backyard may seem harmless, but it's amazing the wide variety of things a dog will eat!

How to Make a Canine First-Aid Kit

If your dog hurts herself, even a minor cut, it can be very upsetting for both of you. Having a first-aid kit handy will help you to help her, calmly and efficiently. What should be in your canine first-aid kit?

- Antibiotic ointment
- Antiseptic and antibacterial cleansing wipes
- Benadryl
- Cotton-tipped applicators
- Disposable razor
- Elastic wrap bandages
- Extra leash and collar
- First-aid tape of various widths
- Gauze bandage roll
- Gauze pads of different sizes, including eye pads
- Hydrogen peroxide
- Instant cold compress
- Kaopectate tablets or liquid
- Latex gloves
- Lubricating jelly
- Muzzle
- Nail clippers
- Pen, pencil, and paper for notes and directions
- Pepto-Bismol
- Round-ended scissors and pointy scissors
- Safety pins
- Sterile saline eyewash
- Thermometer (rectal)
- Tweezers

To induce vomiting, give one teaspoon of 3 percent hydrogen peroxide solution every ten minutes, three times, or place one-half teaspoon of salt at the back of the tongue. Then give the dog one teaspoon per two pounds of body weight of one gram activated charcoal mixed with four cubic centimeters (cc's) of water, if it is available, to delay or prevent the poison from being absorbed.

To speed elimination, thirty minutes later give her one teaspoon of Milk of Magnesia per five pounds of body weight. Then get her to the veterinarian immediately.

Emergency First Aid

Heat Stroke

Heat stroke is characterized by rapid, noisy breathing, a bright red tongue, thick saliva, and sometimes vomiting, plus a high temperature. It requires *immediate* attention. Move the dog immediately to a cooler area. If her temperature is above 104 degrees F, put her in a tub of cool water, hose her down with a garden hose, or give her a cool water enema to bring her temperature down.

Choking

If the dog is choking, place a hard object between her molar teeth on one side of her mouth. With the mouth thus held open, check for any foreign object at the back of the throat or tongue, the roof of the mouth, or between the teeth.

Use long-nose pliers to pull out any foreign object. If you cannot remove it, hold your dog upside down by her hind legs and shake her to dislodge the object. If this does not work, use your fist to exert forceful, sudden pressure on the abdomen at the edge of the breastbone. If the dog is not breathing, administer artificial respiration.

Hypothermia

If your dog is exposed to cold for a prolonged period, particularly if she is wet, she may suffer from hypothermia. Symptoms of hypothermia include violent shivering followed by listlessness, and a temperature below 97 degrees F. Apply warm water packs to the dog's armpits, chest, and stomach, or use a hair dryer set on warm until her temperature reaches 100 degrees F. Then give her honey to increase her blood sugar level.

Why It's Best Not to Breed Your Dog

The discussion of the inherited diseases earlier in this chapter is one reason why only knowledgeable individuals should breed dogs. No one wants to produce unhealthy animals who will die in the nest or cause heartbreak to their owners. Breeding should be done only with the goal of improving the breed's health, conformation, and temperament. It requires a great deal of knowledge and study.

The fact that your Shih Tzu is registered with the AKC does not mean she is a quality representative of the breed; it only means both her parents were registered with the AKC. Most purebred dogs should not be bred, and many responsible

Why Spay and Neuter?

Breeding dogs is a serious undertaking that should only be part of a well-planned breeding program. Why? Because dogs pass on their physical and behavioral problems to their offspring. Even healthy, well-behaved dogs can pass on problems in their genes.

Is your dog so sweet that you'd like to have a litter of puppies just like her? If you breed her to another dog, the pups will not have the same genetic heritage she has. Breeding her *parents* again will increase the odds of a similar pup, but even then, the puppies in the second litter could inherit different genes. In fact, *there is no way to breed a dog to be just like another dog.*

Meanwhile, thousands and thousands of dogs are killed in animal shelters every year simply because they have no homes. Casual breeding is a big contributor to this problem.

If you don't plan to breed your dog, is it still a good idea to spay her or neuter him? Yes!

When you spay your female:

- You avoid her heat cycles, during which she discharges blood and scent.
- It greatly reduces the risk of mammary cancer and eliminates the risk of pyometra (an often fatal infection of the uterus) and uterine cancer.
- It prevents unwanted pregnancies.
- It reduces dominance behaviors and aggression.

When you neuter your male:

- It curbs the desire to roam and to fight with other males.
- It greatly reduces the risk of prostate cancer and eliminates the risk of testicular cancer.
- It helps reduce leg lifting and mounting behavior.
- It reduces dominance behaviors and aggression.

It's impossible to breed a dog to be just like another dog.

breeders sell pet dogs on spay and neuter contracts (withholding registration papers until the surgery is performed) or with AKC limited registration, under which a dog's offspring cannot be registered as purebred.

Whelping a litter can be a joy—or a tragedy. You could wind up losing both puppies and mother, and you are unlikely to make any money after paying for health care, stud fees, puppy food, and advertising the litter. Leave the responsibility and possible pain of breeding to someone more knowledgeable.

Raising a litter successfully takes a lot of time and expertise. Most important, *what will happen to the puppies you have brought into the world?* You may think they have found good homes, but even if they have, what happens if their owners move or divorce, or if a dog you sold becomes ill? Are you willing to take back dogs you have bred?

We all know how many unfortunate dogs wind up put to death at shelters. Most Shih Tzu found in the animal shelters are the result of commercial breeding for wholesaling to pet shops, and casual breeding by uneducated pet owners. Do you want to be responsible for adding to the statistics?

The best thing pet Shih Tzu owners can do for the breed is to have their pets spayed or neutered, for all the reasons outlined in the box on page 95. An altered pet is much easier to live with, and no dog needs to produce puppies to improve her temperament! One litter of puppies will cost you far more than a spay or neuter surgery, so do the right thing—for yourself, your dog, and the breed.

Instead of breeding a litter, why not adopt a rescue dog or serve as a volunteer at your local animal shelter? The American Shih Tzu Club and many local breed clubs are active in Shih Tzu rescue and would welcome your help.

Caring for Your Older Shih Tzu

Shih Tzu are a long-lived breed. Most remain hale and hearty well into their teens. As your dog ages, she will spend more time sleeping. Because she is less active, she should consume fewer calories and still get moderate exercise so that she does not become obese. Her hearing and eyesight may be less keen, her joints may become stiff, and she may need to eliminate more frequently. Maintaining her regular routine as much as possible will give her needed security. If you notice any unusual behavior or symptoms, consult your veterinarian.

Sometimes, if introduced carefully, a young puppy can give an older dog a new lease on life. Just be sure you do not neglect your old friend if you acquire a new puppy. Remember, the puppy has always been used to being one of a crowd, while your older dog needs to know that she still comes first in your life.

Part III

Enjoying Your Shih Tzu

Chapter 9

Training Your Shih Tzu

by Peggy Moran

Training makes your best friend better! A properly trained dog has a happier life and a longer life expectancy. He is also more appreciated by the people he encounters each day, both at home and out and about.

A trained dog walks nicely and joins his family often, going places untrained dogs cannot go. He is never rude or unruly, and he always happily comes when called. When he meets people for the first time, he greets them by sitting and waiting to be petted, rather than jumping up. At home he doesn't compete with his human family, and alone he is not destructive or overly anxious. He isn't continually nagged with words like "no," since he has learned not to misbehave in the first place. He is never shamed, harshly punished, or treated unkindly, and he is a well-loved, involved member of the family.

Sounds good, doesn't it? If you are willing to invest some time, thought, and patience, the words above could soon be used to describe your dog (though perhaps changing "he" to "she"). Educating your pet in a positive way is fun and easy, and there is no better gift you can give your pet than the guarantee of improved understanding and a great relationship.

This chapter will explain how to offer kind leadership, reshape your pet's behavior in a positive and practical way, and even get a head start on simple obedience training.

Understanding Builds the Bond

Dog training is a learning adventure on both ends of the leash. Before attempting to teach their dog new behaviors or change unwanted ones, thoughtful dog owners take the time to understand why their pets behave the way they do, and how their own behavior can be either a positive or negative influence on their dog.

Canine Nature

Loving dogs as much as we do, it's easy to forget they are a completely different species. Despite sharing our homes and living as appreciated members of our families, dogs do not think or learn exactly the same way people do. Even if you love your dog like a child, you must remember to respect the fact that he is actually a dog.

Dogs have no idea when their behavior is inappropriate from a human perspective. They are not aware of the value of possessions they chew or of messes they make or the worry they sometimes seem to cause. While people tend to look at behavior as good and bad or right and wrong, dogs just discover what works and what doesn't work. Then they behave accordingly, learning from their own experiences and increasing or reducing behaviors to improve results for themselves.

You might wonder, "But don't dogs want to please us"? My answer is yes, provided your pleasure reflects back to them in positive ways they can feel and appreciate. Dogs do things for *dog* reasons, and everything they do works for them in some way or they wouldn't be doing it!

The Social Dog

Our pets descended from animals who lived in tightly knit, cooperative social groups. Though far removed in appearance and lifestyle from their ancestors, our dogs still relate in many of the same ways their wild relatives did. And in their relationships with one another, wild canids either lead or follow.

Canine ranking relationships are not about cruelty and power; they are about achievement and abilities. Competent dogs with high levels of drive and confidence step up, while deferring dogs step aside. But followers don't get the short end of the stick; they benefit from the security of having a more competent dog at the helm.

Our domestic dogs still measure themselves against other members of their group—us! Dog owners whose actions lead to positive results have willing, secure followers. But dogs may step up and fill the void or cut loose and do their own thing when their people fail to show capable leadership. When dogs are pushy, aggressive, and rude, or independent and unwilling, it's not because they have designs on the role of "master." It is more likely their owners failed to provide consistent leadership.

Dogs in training benefit from their handler's good leadership. Their education flows smoothly because they are impressed. Being in charge doesn't require you to physically dominate or punish your dog. You simply need to make some subtle changes in the way you relate to him every day.

Lead Your Pack!

Create schedules and structure daily activities. Dogs are creatures of habit, and routines will create security. Feed meals at the same times each day and also try to schedule regular walks, training practices, and toilet outings. Your predictability will help your dog be patient.

Ask your dog to perform a task. Before releasing him to food or freedom, have him do something as simple as sit on command. Teach him that cooperation earns great results!

Give a release prompt (such as "let's go") when going through doors leading outside. This is a better idea than allowing your impatient pup to rush past you.

Pet your dog when he is calm, not when he is excited. Turn your touch into a tool that relaxes and settles.

Reward desirable rather than inappropriate behavior. Petting a jumping dog (who hasn't been invited up) reinforces jumping. Pet sitting dogs, and only invite lap dogs up after they've first "asked" by waiting for your invitation.

Replace personal punishment with positive reinforcement. Show a dog what *to do,* and motivate him to want to do it, and there will be no need to punish him for what he should *not do.* Dogs naturally follow, without the need for force or harshness.

Play creatively and appropriately. Your dog will learn the most about his social rank when he is playing with you. During play, dogs work to control toys and try to get the best of one another in a friendly way. The wrong sorts of play can create problems: For example, tug of war can lead to aggressiveness. Allowing your dog to control toys during play may result in possessive guarding when he has something he really values, such as a bone. Dogs who are chased during play may later run away from you when you approach to leash them. The right kinds of play will help increase your dog's social confidence while you gently assert your leadership.

How Dogs Learn (and How They Don't)

Dog training begins as a meeting of minds—yours and your dog's. Though the end goal may be to get your dog's body to behave in a specific way, training starts as a mind game. Your dog is learning all the time by observing the consequences of his actions and social interactions. He is always seeking out what he perceives as desirable and trying to avoid what he perceives as undesirable.

He will naturally repeat a behavior that either brings him more good stuff or makes bad stuff go away (these are both types of reinforcement). He will naturally avoid a behavior that brings him more bad stuff or makes the good stuff go away (these are both types of punishment).

Both reinforcement and punishment can be perceived as either the direct result of something the dog did himself, or as coming from an outside source.

Using Life's Rewards

Your best friend is smart and he is also cooperative. When the best things in life can only be had by working with you, your dog will view you as a facilitator. You unlock doors to all of the positively reinforcing experiences he values: his freedom, his friends at the park, food, affection, walks, and play. The trained dog accompanies you through those doors and waits to see what working with you will bring.

Rewarding your dog for good behavior is called positive reinforcement, and, as we've just seen, it increases the likelihood that he will repeat that behavior. The perfect reward is anything your dog wants that is safe and appropriate. Don't limit yourself to toys, treats, and things that come directly from you. Harness life's positives—barking at squirrels, chasing a falling leaf, bounding away from you at the dog park, pausing for a moment to sniff everything—and allow your dog to earn access to those things as rewards that come from cooperating with you. When he looks at you, when he sits, when he comes when you call—any prompted behavior can earn one of life's rewards. When he works with you, he earns the things he most appreciates; but when he tries to get those things on his own, he cannot. Rather than seeing you as someone who always says "no," your dog will view you as the one who says "let's go!" He will *want* to follow.

What About Punishment?

Not only is it unnecessary to personally punish dogs, it is abusive. No matter how convinced you are that your dog "knows right from wrong," in reality he will associate personal punishment with the punisher. The resulting cowering, "guilty"-looking postures are actually displays of submission and fear. Later,

Purely Positive Reinforcement

With positive training, we emphasize teaching dogs what they should do to earn reinforcements, rather than punishing them for unwanted behaviors.

- Focus on teaching "do" rather than "don't." For example, a sitting dog isn't jumping.
- Use positive reinforcers that are valuable to your dog and the situation: A tired dog values rest; a confined dog values freedom.
- Play (appropriately)!
- Be a consistent leader.
- Set your dog up for success by anticipating and preventing problems.
- Notice and reward desirable behavior, and give him lots of attention when he is being good.
- Train ethically. Use humane methods and equipment that do not frighten or hurt your dog.
- When you are angry, walk away and plan a positive strategy.
- Keep practice sessions short and sweet. Five to ten minutes, three to five times a day is best.

when the punisher isn't around and the coast is clear, the same behavior he was punished for—such as raiding a trash can—might bring a self-delivered, very tasty result. The punished dog hasn't learned not to misbehave; he has learned to not get caught.

Does punishment ever have a place in dog training? Many people will heartily insist it does not. But dog owners often get frustrated as they try to stick to the path of all-positive reinforcement. It sure sounds great, but is it realistic, or even natural, to *never* say "no" to your dog?

A wild dog's life is not *all* positive. Hunger and thirst are both examples of negative reinforcement; the resulting discomfort motivates the wild dog to seek food and water. He encounters natural aversives such as pesky insects; mats in his coat; cold days; rainy days; sweltering hot days; and occasional run-ins with thorns, brambles, skunks, bees, and other nastiness. These all affect his behavior, as he tries to avoid the bad stuff whenever possible. The wild dog also occasionally encounters social punishers from others in his group when he gets too pushy. Starting with a growl or a snap from Mom, and later some mild and ritualized discipline from other members of his four-legged family, he learns to modify behaviors that elicit grouchy responses.

Our pet dogs don't naturally experience all positive results either, because they learn from their surroundings and from social experiences with other dogs. Watch a group of pet dogs playing together and you'll see a very old educational system still being used. As they wrestle and attempt to assert themselves, you'll notice many mouth-on-neck moments. Their playful biting is inhibited, with no intention to cause harm, but their message is clear: "Say uncle or this could hurt more!"

Observing that punishment does occur in nature, some people may feel compelled to try to be like the big wolf with their pet dogs. Becoming aggressive or heavy-handed with your pet will backfire! Your dog will not be impressed, nor will he want to follow you. Punishment causes dogs to change their behavior to avoid or escape discomfort and threats. Threatened dogs will either become very passive and offer submissive, appeasing postures, attempt to flee, or rise to the occasion and fight back. When people personally punish their dogs in an angry manner, one of these three defensive mechanisms will be triggered. Which one depends on a dog's genetic temperament as well as his past social experiences. Since we don't want to make our pets feel the need to avoid or escape us, personal punishment has no place in our training.

Remote Consequences

Sometimes, however, all-positive reinforcement is just not enough. That's because not all reinforcement comes from us. An inappropriate behavior can be self-reinforcing—just doing it makes the dog feel better in some way, whether you are there to say "good boy!" or not. Some examples are eating garbage, pulling the stuffing out of your sofa, barking at passersby, or urinating on the floor.

Although you don't want to personally punish your dog, the occasional deterrent may be called for to help derail these kinds of self-rewarding misbehaviors. In these cases, mild forms of impersonal or remote punishment can be used as part of a correction. The goal isn't to make your dog feel bad or to "know he has done wrong," but to help redirect him to alternate behaviors that are more acceptable to you.

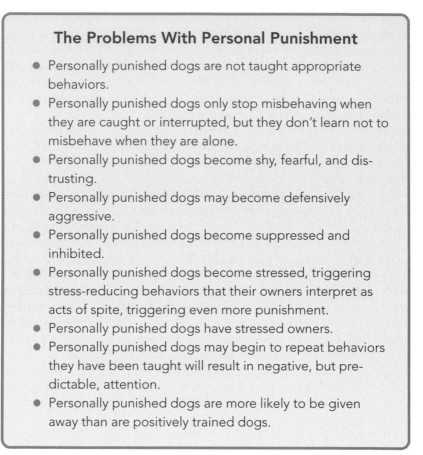

The Problems With Personal Punishment

- Personally punished dogs are not taught appropriate behaviors.
- Personally punished dogs only stop misbehaving when they are caught or interrupted, but they don't learn not to misbehave when they are alone.
- Personally punished dogs become shy, fearful, and distrusting.
- Personally punished dogs may become defensively aggressive.
- Personally punished dogs become suppressed and inhibited.
- Personally punished dogs become stressed, triggering stress-reducing behaviors that their owners interpret as acts of spite, triggering even more punishment.
- Personally punished dogs have stressed owners.
- Personally punished dogs may begin to repeat behaviors they have been taught will result in negative, but predictable, attention.
- Personally punished dogs are more likely to be given away than are positively trained dogs.

You do this by pairing a slightly startling, totally impersonal sound with an equally impersonal and *very mild* remote consequence. The impersonal sound might be a single shake of an empty plastic pop bottle with pennies in it, held out of your dog's sight. Or you could use a vocal expression such as "eh!" delivered with you looking *away* from your misbehaving dog.

Pair your chosen sound—the penny bottle or "eh!"—with either a slight tug on his collar or a sneaky spritz on the rump from a water bottle. Do this right *as* he touches something he should not; bad timing will confuse your dog and undermine your training success.

To keep things under your control and make sure you get the timing right, it's best to do this as a setup. "Accidentally" drop a shoe on the floor, and then help your dog learn some things are best avoided. As he sniffs the shoe say "eh!" without looking at him and give a *slight* tug against his collar. This sound will quickly become meaningful as a correction all by itself—sometimes after just one setup—making the tug correction obsolete. The tug lets your dog see that you were right; going for that shoe *was* a bad idea! Your wise dog will be more likely to heed your warning next time, and probably move closer to you where it's safe. Be a good friend and pick up the nasty shoe. He'll be relieved and you'll look heroic. Later, when he's home alone and encounters a stray shoe, he'll want to give it a wide berth.

Your negative marking sound will come in handy in the future, when your dog begins to venture down the wrong behavioral path. The goal is not to announce your disapproval or to threaten your dog. You are not telling him to stop or showing how *you* feel about his behavior. You are sounding a warning to a friend who's venturing off toward danger—"I wouldn't if I were you!" Suddenly, there is an abrupt, rather startling, noise! Now is the moment to redirect him and help him earn positive reinforcement. That interrupted behavior will become something he wants to avoid in the future, but he won't want to avoid you.

Practical Commands for Family Pets

Before you begin training your dog, let's look at some equipment you'll want to have on hand:

- **A buckle collar** is fine for most dogs. *Do not* use a choke chain (sometimes called a training collar), because they cause physical harm even when used correctly.
- **Six-foot training leash and twenty-six–foot retractable leash.**
- **A few empty plastic soda bottles with about twenty pennies in each one.** This will be used to impersonally interrupt misbehaviors before redirecting dogs to more positive activities.
- **A favorite squeaky toy,** to motivate, attract attention, and reward your dog during training.

Lure your dog to take just a few steps with you on the leash by being inviting and enthusiastic. Make sure you reward him for his efforts.

Baby Steps

Allow your young pup to drag a short, lightweight leash attached to a buckle collar for a few *supervised* moments, several times each day. At first the leash may annoy him and he may jump around a bit trying to get away from it. Distract him with your squeaky toy or a bit of his kibble and he'll quickly get used to his new "tail."

Begin walking him on the leash by holding the end and following him. As he adapts, you can begin to assert gentle direct pressure to teach him to follow you. Don't jerk or yank, or he will become afraid to walk when the leash is on. If he becomes hesitant, squat down facing him and let him figure out that by moving toward you he is safe and secure. If he remains confused or frightened and doesn't come to you, go to him and help him understand that you provide safe harbor while he's on the leash. Then back away a few steps and try again to lure him to you. As he learns that you are the "home base," he'll want to follow when you walk a few steps, waiting for you to stop, squat down, and make him feel great.

So Attached to You!

The next step in training your dog—and this is a very important one—is to begin spending at least an hour or more each day with him on a four- to six-foot leash, held by or tethered to you. This training will increase his attachment to you—literally!—as you sit quietly or walk about, tending to your household business. When you are quiet, he'll learn it is time to settle; when you are active, he'll learn to move with you. Tethering also keeps him out of trouble when you are busy but still want his company. It is a great alternative to confining a dog, and can be used instead of crating any time you're home and need to slow him down a bit.

Rotating your dog from supervised freedom to tethered time to some quiet time in the crate or his gated area gives him a diverse and balanced day while he is learning. Two confined or tethered hours is the most you should require of your dog in one stretch, before changing to some supervised freedom, play, or a walk.

The dog in training may, at times, be stressed by all of the changes he is dealing with. Provide a stress outlet, such as a toy to chew on, when he is confined or tethered. He will settle into his quiet time more quickly and completely. Always be sure to provide several rounds of daily play and free time (in a fenced area or on your retractable leash) in addition to plenty of chewing materials.

Tethering your dog is a great way to keep him calm and under control, but still with you.

Dog Talk

Dogs don't speak in words, but they do have a language—body language. They use postures, vocalizations, movements, facial gestures, odors, and touch— usually with their mouths—to communicate what they are feeling and thinking.

We also "speak" using body language. We have quite an array of postures, movements, and facial gestures that accompany our touch and language as we attempt to communicate with our pets. And our dogs can quickly figure us out!

Alone, without associations, words are just noises. But, because we pair them with meaningful body language, our dogs make the connection. Dogs can really learn to understand much of what we *say*, if what we *do* at the same time is consistent.

The Positive Marker

Start your dog's education with one of the best tricks in dog training: Pair various positive reinforcers—food, a toy, touch—with a sound such as a click on a clicker (which you can get at the pet supply store) or a spoken word like "good!" or "yes!" This will enable you to later "mark" your dog's desirable behaviors.

It seems too easy: Just say "yes!" and give the dog his toy. (Or use whatever sound and reward you have chosen.) Later, when you make your marking sound right at the instant your dog does the right thing, he will know you are going to be giving him something good for that particular action. And he'll be eager to repeat the behavior to hear you mark it again!

Next, you must teach your dog to understand the meaning of cues you'll be using to ask him to perform specific behaviors. This is easy, too. Does he already do things you might like him to do on command? Of course! He lies down, he sits, he picks things up, he drops them again, he comes to you. All of the behaviors you'd like to control are already part of your dog's natural repertoire. The trick is getting him to offer those behaviors when you ask for them. And that means you have to teach him to associate a particular behavior on his part with a particular behavior on your part.

Sit Happens

Teach your dog an important new rule: From now on, he is only touched and petted when he is either sitting or lying down. You won't need to ask him to sit; in fact, you should not. Just keeping him tethered near you so there isn't much to do but stand, be ignored, or settle, and wait until sit happens.

He may pester you a bit, but be stoic and unresponsive. Starting now, when *you* are sitting down, a sitting dog is the only one you see and pay attention to. He will eventually sit, and as he does, attach the word "sit"—but don't be too excited or he'll jump right back up. Now mark with your positive sound that promises something good, then reward him with a slow, quiet, settling pet.

Training requires consistent reinforcement. Ask others to also wait until your dog is sitting and calm to touch him, and he will associate being petted with being relaxed. Be sure you train your dog to associate everyone's touch with quiet bonding.

Reinforcing "Sit" as a Command

Since your dog now understands one concept of working for a living—sit to earn petting—you can begin to shape and reinforce his desire to sit. Hold toys, treats, his bowl of food, and turn into a statue. But don't prompt him to sit! Instead, remain frozen and unavailable, looking somewhere out into space, over his head. He will put on a bit of a show, trying to get a response from you, and may offer various behaviors, but only one will push your button—sitting. Wait for him to offer the "right" behavior, and when he does, you unfreeze. Say "sit," then mark with an excited "good!" and give him the toy or treat with a release command—"OK!"

When you notice spontaneous sits occurring, be sure to take advantage of those free opportunities to make your command sequence meaningful and positive. Say "sit" as you observe sit happen—then mark with "good!" and praise, pet, or reward the dog. Soon, every time you look at your dog he'll be sitting and looking right back at you!

Now, after thirty days of purely positive practice, it's time to give him a test. When he is just walking around doing his own thing, suddenly ask him to sit. He'll probably do it right away. If he doesn't, do *not* repeat your command, or you'll just undermine its meaning ("sit" means sit *now;* the command is not "sit, sit, sit, sit"). Instead, get something he likes and let him know you have it. Wait for him to offer the sit—he will—then say "sit!" and complete your marking and rewarding sequence.

OK

"OK" will probably rate as one of your dog's favorite words. It's like the word "recess" to schoolchildren. It is the word used to release your dog from a command. You can introduce "OK" during your "sit" practice. When he gets up from a sit, say "OK" to tell him the sitting is finished. Soon that sound will mean "freedom."

Make it even more meaningful and positive. Whenever he spontaneously bounds away, say "OK!" Squeak a toy, and when he notices and shows interest, toss it for him.

Down

I've mentioned that you should only pet your dog when he is either sitting or lying down. Now, using the approach I've just introduced for "sit," teach your dog to lie down. You will be a statue, and hold something he would like to get but that you'll only release to a dog who is lying down. It helps to lower the desired item to the floor in front of him, still not speaking and not letting him have it until he offers you the new behavior you are seeking.

Lower your dog's reward to the floor to help him figure out what behavior will earn him his reward.

He may offer a sit and then wait expectantly, but you must make him keep searching for the new trick that triggers your generosity. Allow your dog to experiment and find the right answer, even if he has to search around for it first. When he lands on "down" and learns it is another behavior that works, he'll offer it more quickly the next time.

Don't say "down" until he lies down, to tightly associate your prompt with the correct behavior. To say "down, down, down" as he is sitting, looking at you, or pawing at the toy would make "down" mean those behaviors instead! Whichever behavior he offers, a training opportunity has been created. Once you've attached and shaped both sitting and lying down, you can ask for both behaviors with your verbal prompts, "sit" or "down." Be sure to only reinforce the "correct" reply!

Stay

"Stay" can easily be taught as an extension of what you've already been practicing. To teach "stay," you follow the entire sequence for reinforcing a "sit" or "down," except you wait a bit longer before you give the release word, "OK!" Wait a second or two longer during each practice before saying "OK!" and releasing your dog to the positive reinforcer (toy, treat, or one of life's other rewards).

You can step on the leash to help your dog understand the down-stay, but only do this when he is already lying down. You don't want to hurt him!

If he gets up before you've said "OK," you have two choices: pretend the release was your idea and quickly interject "OK!" as he breaks; or, if he is more experienced and practiced, mark the behavior with your correction sound— "eh!"— and then gently put him back on the spot, wait for him to lie down, and begin again. Be sure the next three practices are a success. Ask him to wait for just a second, and release him before he can be wrong. You need to keep your dog feeling like more of a success than a failure as you begin to test his training in increasingly more distracting and difficult situations.

As he gets the hang of it—he stays until you say "OK"— you can gradually push for longer times—up to a minute on a sit-stay, and up to three minutes on a down-stay. You can also gradually add distractions and work in new environments. To add a minor self-correction for the down-stay, stand on the dog's leash after he lies down, allowing about three inches of slack. If tries to get up before you've said "OK," he'll discover it doesn't work.

Do not step on the leash to make your dog lie down! This could badly hurt his neck, and will destroy his trust in you. Remember, we are teaching our dogs to make the best choices, not inflicting our answers upon them!

Come

Rather than thinking of "come" as an action—"come to me"—think of it as a place—"the dog is sitting in front of me, facing me." Since your dog by now really likes sitting to earn your touch and other positive reinforcement, he's likely to sometimes sit directly in front of you, facing you, all on his own. When this happens, give it a specific name: "come."

Now follow the rest of the training steps you have learned to make him like doing it and reinforce the behavior by practicing it any chance you get. Anything your dog wants and likes could be earned as a result of his first offering the sit-in-front known as "come."

You can help guide him into the right location. Use your hands as "landing gear" and pat the insides of your legs at his nose level. Do this while backing up a bit, to help him maneuver to the straight-in-front, facing-you position. Don't say the word "come" while he's maneuvering,

Pat the insides of your legs to show your dog exactly where you like him to sit when you say "come."

because he hasn't! You are trying to make "come" the end result, not the work in progress.

You can also help your dog by marking his movement in the right direction: Use your positive sound or word to promise he is getting warm. When he finally sits facing you, enthusiastically say "come," mark again with your positive word, and release him with an enthusiastic "OK!" Make it so worth his while, with lots of play and praise, that he can't wait for you to ask him to come again!

Building a Better Recall

Practice, practice, practice. Now, practice some more. Teach your dog that all good things in life hinge upon him first sitting in front of you in a behavior named "come." When you think he really has got it, test him by asking him to "come" as you gradually add distractions and change locations. Expect setbacks as you make these changes and practice accordingly. Lower your expectations and make his task easier so he is able to get it right. Use those distractions as rewards, when they are appropriate. For example, let him check out the interesting leaf that blew by as a reward for first coming to you and ignoring it.

Add distance and call your dog to come while he is on his retractable leash. If he refuses and sits looking at you blankly, *do not* jerk, tug, "pop," or reel him in. Do nothing! It is his move; wait to see what behavior he offers. He'll either begin to approach (mark the behavior with an excited "good!"), sit and do nothing (just keep waiting), or he'll try to move in some direction other than toward you. If he tries to leave, use your correction marker—"eh!"—and bring him to a stop by letting him walk to the end of the leash, *not* by jerking him. Now walk to him in a neutral manner, and don't jerk or show any disapproval. Gently bring him back to the spot where he was when you called him, then back away and face him, still waiting and not reissuing your command. Let him keep examining his options until he finds the one that works—yours!

If you have practiced everything I've suggested so far and given your dog a chance to really learn what "come" means, he is well aware of what you want and is quite intelligently weighing all his options. The only way he'll know your way is the one that works is to be allowed to examine his other choices and discover that they *don't* work.

Sooner or later every dog tests his training. Don't be offended or angry when your dog tests you. No matter how positive you've made it, he won't always want to do everything you ask, every time. When he explores the "what happens if I don't" scenario, your training is being strengthened. He will discover through his own process of trial and error that the best—and only—way out of a command he really doesn't feel compelled to obey is to obey it.

Let's Go

Many pet owners wonder if they can retain control while walking their dogs and still allow at least some running in front, sniffing, and playing. You might worry that allowing your dog occasional freedom could result in him expecting it all the time, leading to a testy, leash-straining walk. It's possible for both parties on the leash to have an enjoyable experience by implementing and reinforcing well-thought-out training techniques.

Begin by making word associations you'll use on your walks. Give the dog some slack on the leash, and as he starts to walk away from you say "OK" and begin to follow him.

Do not let him drag you; set the pace even when he is being given a turn at being the leader. Whenever he starts to pull, just come to a standstill and refuse to move (or refuse to allow him to continue forward) until there is slack in the leash. Do this correction without saying anything at all. When he isn't pulling, you may decide to just stand still and let him sniff about within the range the slack leash allows, or you may even mosey along following him. After a few minutes of "recess," it is time to work. Say something like "that's it" or "time's up," close the distance between you and your dog, and touch him.

Next say "let's go" (or whatever command you want to use to mean "follow me as we walk"). Turn and walk off, and, if he follows, mark his behavior with "good!" Then stop,

Give your dog slack on his leash as you walk and let him make the decision to walk with you.

When your dog catches up with you, make sure you let him know what a great dog he is!

Intersperse periods of attentive walking, where your dog is on a shorter leash, with periods on a slack leash, where he is allowed to look and sniff around.

squat down, and let him catch you. Make him glad he did! Start again, and do a few transitions as he gets the hang of your follow-the-leader game, speeding up, slowing down, and trying to make it fun. When you stop, he gets to catch up and receive some deserved positive reinforcement. Don't forget that's the reason he is following you, so be sure to make it worth his while!

Require him to remain attentive to you. Do not allow sniffing, playing, eliminating, or pulling during your time as leader on a walk. If he seems to get distracted—which, by the way, is the main reason dogs walk poorly with their people—change direction or pace without saying a word. Just help him realize "oops, I lost track of my human." Do not jerk his neck and say "heel"—this will make the word "heel" mean pain in the neck and will not encourage him to cooperate with you. Don't repeat "let's go," either. He needs to figure out that it is his job to keep track of and follow you if he wants to earn the positive benefits you provide.

The best reward you can give a dog for performing an attentive, controlled walk is a few minutes of walking without all of the controls. Of course, he must remain on a leash even during the "recess" parts of the walk, but allowing him to discriminate between attentive following—"let's go"—and having a few moments of relaxation—"OK"—will increase his willingness to work.

Training for Attention

Your dog pretty much has a one-track mind. Once he is focused on something, everything else is excluded. This can be great, for instance, when he's focusing on you! But it can also be dangerous if, for example, his attention is riveted on the bunny he is chasing and he does not hear you call—that is, not unless he has been trained to pay attention when you say his name.

When you say your dog's name, you'll want him to make eye contact with you. Begin teaching this by making yourself so intriguing that he can't help but look.

When you call your dog's name, you will again be seeking a specific response—eye contact. The best way to teach this is to trigger his alerting response by making a noise with your mouth, such as whistling or a kissing sound, and then immediately doing something he'll find very intriguing.

You can play a treasure hunt game to help teach him to regard his name as a request for attention. As a bonus, you can reinforce the rest of his new vocabulary at the same time.

Treasure Hunt

Make a kissing sound, then jump up and find a dog toy or dramatically raid the fridge and rather noisily eat a piece of cheese. After doing this twice, make a kissing sound and then look at your dog.

Of course he is looking at you! He is waiting to see if that sound—the kissing sound—means you're going to go hunting again. After all, you're so good at it! Because he is looking, say his name, mark with "good," then go hunting and find his toy. Release it to him with an "OK." At any point if he follows you, attach your "let's go!" command; if he leaves you, give permission with "OK."

Using this approach, he cannot be wrong—any behavior your dog offers can be named. You can add things like "take it" when he picks up a toy, and "thank you" when he happens to drop one. Many opportunities to make your new vocabulary meaningful and positive can be found within this simple training game.

Problems to watch out for when teaching the treasure hunt:

- You really do not want your dog to come to you when you call his name (later, when you try to engage his attention to ask him to stay, he'll already be on his way toward you). You just want him to look at you.
- Saying "watch me, watch me" doesn't teach your dog to *offer* his attention. It just makes you a background noise.
- Don't lure your dog's attention with the reward. Get his attention and then reward him for looking. Try holding a toy in one hand with your arm stretched out to your side. Wait until he looks at you rather than the toy. Now say his name then mark with "good!" and release the toy. As he goes for it, say "OK."

To get your dog's attention, try holding his toy with your arm out to your side. Wait until he looks at you, then mark the moment and give him the toy.

Teaching Cooperation

Never punish your dog for failing to obey you or try to punish him into compliance. Bribing, repeating yourself, and doing a behavior for him all avoid the real issue of dog training—his will. He must be helped to be willing, not made to achieve tasks. Good dog training helps your dog want to obey. He learns that he can gain what he values most through cooperation and compliance, and can't gain those things any other way.

Your dog is learning to *earn,* rather than expect, the good things in life. And you've become much more important to him than you were before. Because you are allowing him to experiment and learn, he doesn't have to be forced, manipulated, or bribed. When he wants something, he can gain it by cooperating with you. One of those "somethings"—and a great reward you shouldn't underestimate—is your positive attention, paid to him with love and sincere approval!

Chapter 10

Housetraining Your Shih Tzu

Excerpted from Housetraining: An Owner's Guide to a Happy Healthy Pet, 1st Edition, *by September Morn*

By the time puppies are about 3 weeks old, they start to follow their mother around. When they are a few steps away from their clean sleeping area, the mama dog stops. The pups try to nurse, but Mom won't allow it. The pups mill around in frustration, then nature calls and they all urinate and defecate here, away from their bed. The mother dog returns to the nest, with her brood waddling behind her. Their first housetraining lesson has been a success.

The next one to housetrain puppies should be their breeder. The breeder watches as the puppies eliminate, then deftly removes the soiled papers and replaces them with clean papers before the pups can traipse back through their messes. He has wisely arranged the puppies' space so their bed, food, and drinking water are as far away from the elimination area as possible. This way, when the pups follow their mama, they will move away from their sleeping and eating area before eliminating. This habit will help the pups be easily housetrained.

Your Housetraining Shopping List

While your puppy's mother and breeder are getting her started on good housetraining habits, you'll need to do some shopping. If you have all the essentials in place before your dog arrives, it will be easier to help her learn the rules from day one.

Newspaper: The younger your puppy and larger her breed, the more newspapers you'll need. Newspaper is absorbent, abundant, cheap, and convenient.

Puddle Pads: If you prefer not to stockpile newspaper, a commercial alternative is puddle pads. These thick paper pads can be purchased under several trade names at pet supply stores. The pads have waterproof backing, so puppy urine doesn't seep through onto the floor. Their disadvantages are that they will cost you more than newspapers and that they contain plastics that are not biodegradable.

Poop Removal Tool: There are several types of poop removal tools available. Some are designed with a separate pan and rake, and others have the handles hinged like scissors. Some scoops need two hands for operation, while others are designed for one-handed use. Try out the different brands at your pet supply store. Put a handful of pebbles or dog kibble on the floor and then pick them up with each type of scoop to determine which works best for you.

Plastic Bags: When you take your dog outside your yard, you *must* pick up after her. Dog waste is unsightly, smelly, and can harbor disease. In many cities and towns, the law mandates dog owners clean up pet waste deposited on public ground. Picking up after your dog using a plastic bag scoop is simple. Just put your hand inside the bag, like a mitten, and then grab the droppings. Turn the bag inside out, tie the top, and that's that.

Crate: To housetrain a puppy, you will need some way to confine her when you're unable to supervise. A dog crate is a secure way to confine your dog for short periods during the day and to use as a comfortable bed at night. Crates come in wire mesh and in plastic. The wire ones are foldable to store flat in a smaller space. The plastic ones are more cozy, draft-free, and quiet, and are approved for airline travel.

Baby Gates: Since you shouldn't crate a dog for more than an hour or two at a time during the day, baby gates are a good way to limit your dog's freedom in the house. Be sure the baby gates you use are safe. The old-fashioned wooden, expanding lattice type has seriously injured a number of children by collapsing and trapping a leg, arm, or neck. That type of gate can hurt a puppy, too, so use the modern grid type gates instead. You'll need more than one baby gate if you have several doorways to close off.

Exercise Pen: Portable exercise pens are great when you have a young pup or a small dog. These metal or plastic pens are made of rectangular panels that are hinged together. The pens are freestanding, sturdy, foldable, and can be carried like a suitcase. You could set one up in your kitchen as the pup's daytime corral, and then take it outdoors to contain your pup while you garden or just sit and enjoy the day.

Enzymatic Cleaner: All dogs make housetraining mistakes. Accept this and be ready for it by buying an enzymatic cleaner made especially for pet accidents. Dogs like to eliminate where they have done it before, and lingering smells lead them to those spots. Ordinary household cleaners may remove all the odors you can smell, but only an enzymatic cleaner will remove everything your dog can smell.

The First Day

Housetraining is a matter of establishing good habits in your dog. That means you never want her to learn anything she will eventually have to unlearn. Start off housetraining on the right foot by teaching your dog that you prefer her to eliminate outside. Designate a potty area in your backyard (if you have one) or in the street in front of your home and take your dog to it as soon as you arrive home. Let her sniff a bit and, when she squats to go, give the action a name: "potty" or "do it" or anything else you won't be embarrassed to say in public. Eventually your dog will associate that word with the act and will eliminate on command. When she's finished, praise her with "good potty!"

Your puppy's mom gave her housetraining lessons starting at about 3 weeks old. You can capitalize on those early lessons by reinforcing good habits and never letting her establish bad ones.

That first day, take your puppy out to the potty area frequently. Although she may not eliminate every time, you are establishing a routine: You take her to her spot, ask her to eliminate, and praise her when she does.

Don't Overuse the Crate

A crate serves well as a dog's overnight bed, but you should not leave the dog in her crate for more than an hour or two during the day. Throughout the day, she needs to play and exercise. She is likely to want to drink some water and will undoubtedly eliminate. Confining your dog all day will give her no option but to soil her crate. This is not just unpleasant for you and the dog, but it reinforces bad cleanliness habits. And crating a pup for the whole day is abusive. Don't do it.

Just before bedtime, take your dog to her potty area once more. Stand by and wait until she produces. Do not put your dog to bed for the night until she has eliminated. Be patient and calm. This is not the time to play with or excite your dog. If she's too excited, a pup not only won't eliminate, she probably won't want to sleep either.

Most dogs, even young ones, will not soil their beds if they can avoid it. For this reason, a sleeping crate can be a tremendous help during housetraining. Being crated at night can help a dog develop the muscles that control elimination. So after your dog has emptied out, put her to bed in her crate.

A good place to put your dog's sleeping crate is near your own bed. Dogs are pack animals, so they feel safer sleeping with others in a common area. In your bedroom, the pup will be near you and you'll be close enough to hear when she wakes during the night and needs to eliminate.

Pups under 4 months old often are not able to hold their urine all night. If your puppy has settled down to sleep but awakens and fusses a few hours later, she probably needs to go out. For the best housetraining progress, take your pup to her elimination area whenever she needs to go, even in the wee hours of the morning.

Your pup may soil in her crate if you ignore her late night urgency. It's unfair to let this happen, and it sends the wrong message about your expectations for cleanliness. Resign yourself to this midnight outing and just get up and take the pup out. Your pup will outgrow this need soon and will learn in the process that she can count on you, and you'll wake happily each morning to a clean dog.

The next morning, the very first order of business is to take your pup out to eliminate. Don't forget to take her to her special potty spot, ask her to eliminate, and then praise her when she does. After your pup empties out in the morning, give her breakfast, and then take her to her potty area again. After that, she shouldn't need to eliminate again right away, so you can allow her some free playtime. Keep an eye on the pup though, because when she pauses in play she may need to go potty. Take her to the right spot, give the command, and praise if she produces.

Confine Your Pup

A pup or dog who has not finished housetraining should *never* be allowed the run of the house unattended. A new dog (especially a puppy) with unlimited access to your house will make her own choices about where to eliminate. Vigilance during your new dog's first few weeks in your home will pay big dividends. Every potty mistake delays housetraining progress; every success speeds it along.

Prevent problems by setting up a controlled environment for your new pet. A good place for a puppy corral is often the kitchen. Kitchens almost always have waterproof or easily cleaned floors, which is a distinct asset with leaky pups. A bathroom, laundry room, or enclosed porch could be used for a puppy corral, but the kitchen is generally the best location. Kitchens are a meeting place and a

Confinement is one of the most important aspects of housetraining. Unlimited access to the house means unlimited choices about where to eliminate.

hub of activity for many families, and a puppy will learn better manners when she is socialized thoroughly with family, friends, and nice strangers.

The way you structure your pup's corral area is very important. Her bed, food, and water should be at the opposite end of the corral from the potty area. When you first get your pup, spread newspaper over the rest of the floor of her playpen corral. Lay the papers at least four pages thick and be sure to overlap the edges. As you note the pup's progress, you can remove the papers nearest the sleeping and eating corner. Gradually decrease the size of the papered area until only the end where you want the pup to eliminate is covered. If you will be training your dog to eliminate outside, place newspaper at the end of the corral that is closest to the door that leads outdoors. That way as she moves away from the clean area to the papered area, the pup will also form the habit of heading toward the door to go out.

> ### TIP
> **Water**
> Make sure your dog has access to clean water at all times. Limiting the amount of water a dog drinks is not necessary for housetraining success and can be very dangerous. A dog needs water to digest food, to maintain a proper body temperature and proper blood volume, and to clean her system of toxins and wastes. A healthy dog will automatically drink the right amount. Do not restrict water intake. Controlling your dog's access to water is not the key to housetraining her; controlling her access to everything else in your home is.

Maintain a scent marker for the pup's potty area by reserving a small soiled piece of paper when you clean up. Place this piece, with her scent of urine, under the top sheet of the clean papers you spread. This will cue your pup where to eliminate.

Most dog owners use a combination of indoor papers and outdoor elimination areas. When the pup is left by herself in the corral, she can potty on the ever-present newspaper. When you are available to take the pup outside, she can do her business in the outdoor spot. It is not difficult to switch a pup from indoor paper training to outdoor elimination. Owners of large pups often switch early, but potty papers are still useful if the pup spends time in her indoor corral while you're away. Use the papers as long as your pup needs them. If you come home and they haven't been soiled, you are ahead.

When setting up your pup's outdoor yard, put the lounging area as far away as possible from the potty area, just as with the indoor corral setup. People with large yards, for example, might leave a patch unmowed at the edge of the lawn to serve as the dog's elimination area. Other dog owners teach the dog to relieve herself in a designated corner of a deck or patio. For an apartment-dwelling city

City dogs will need to learn to eliminate out in the street. It's no problem for your smart Shih Tzu!

dog, the outdoor potty area might be a tiny balcony or the curb. Each dog owner has somewhat different expectations for their dog. Teach your dog to eliminate in a spot that suits your environment and lifestyle.

Be sure to pick up droppings in your yard at least once a day. Dogs have a natural desire to stay far away from their own excrement, and if too many piles litter the ground, your dog won't want to walk through it and will start eliminating elsewhere. Leave just one small piece of feces in the potty area to remind your dog where the right spot is located.

To help a pup adapt to the change from indoors to outdoors, take one of her potty papers outside to the new elimination area. Let the pup stand on the paper when she goes potty outdoors. Each day for four days, reduce the size of the paper by half. By the fifth day, the pup, having used a smaller and smaller piece of paper to stand on, will probably just go to that spot and eliminate.

Take your pup to her outdoor potty place frequently throughout the day. A puppy can hold her urine for only about as many hours as her age in months, and will move her bowels as many times a day as she eats. So a 2-month-old pup will urinate about every two hours, while at 4 months she can manage about four hours between piddles. Pups vary somewhat in their rate of development, so this is not a hard and fast rule. It does, however, present a realistic idea of how long a pup can be left without access to a potty place. Past 4 months, her potty trips will be less frequent.

When you take the dog outdoors to her spot, keep her leashed so that she won't wander away. Stand quietly and let her sniff around in the designated area. If your pup starts to leave before she has eliminated, gently lead her back and remind her to go. If your pup sniffs at the spot, praise her calmly, say the command word, and just wait. If she produces, praise serenely, then give her time to sniff around a little more. She may not be finished, so give her time to go again before allowing her to play and explore her new home.

If you find yourself waiting more than five minutes for your dog to potty, take her back inside. Watch your pup carefully for twenty minutes, not giving her any opportunity to slip away to eliminate unnoticed. If you are too busy to watch the pup, put her in her crate. After twenty minutes, take her to the outdoor potty spot again and tell her what to do. If you're unsuccessful after five minutes, crate the dog again. Give her another chance to eliminate in fifteen or twenty minutes. Eventually, she will have to go.

Watch Your Pup

Be vigilant and don't let the pup make a mistake in the house. Each time you successfully anticipate elimination and take your pup to the potty spot, you'll move a step closer to your goal. Stay aware of your puppy's needs. If you ignore the pup, she will make mistakes and you'll be cleaning up more messes.

Keep a chart of your new dog's elimination behavior for the first three or four days. Jot down what times she eats, sleeps, and eliminates. After several days a pattern will emerge that can help you determine your pup's body rhythms. Most dogs tend to eliminate at fairly regular intervals. Once you know your new dog's natural rhythms, you'll be able to anticipate her needs and schedule appropriate potty outings.

Understanding the meanings of your dog's postures can also help you win the battle of the puddle. When your dog is getting ready to eliminate, she will display a specific set of postures. The sooner you can learn to read these signals, the cleaner your floor will stay.

A young puppy who feels the urge to eliminate may start to sniff the ground and walk in a circle. If the pup is very young, she may simply squat and go. All young puppies,

Backyard potty breaks should be all business. Don't let your pup turn them into playtime.

Watch your puppy closely for signs that she needs to go out, and remember that accidents happen.

male or female, squat to urinate. If you are housetraining a pup under 4 months of age, regardless of sex, watch for the beginnings of a squat as the signal to rush the pup to the potty area.

When a puppy is getting ready to defecate, she may run urgently back and forth or turn in a circle while sniffing or starting to squat. If defecation is imminent, the pup's anus may protrude or open slightly. When she starts to go, the pup will squat and hunch her back, her tail sticking straight out behind. There is no mistaking this posture; nothing else looks like this. If your pup takes this position, take her to her potty area. Hurry! You may have to carry her to get there in time.

A young puppy won't have much time between feeling the urge and actually eliminating, so you'll have to be quick to note her postural clues and intercept your pup in time. Pups from 3 to 6 months have a few seconds more between the urge and the act than younger ones do. The older your pup, the more time you'll have to get her to the potty area after she begins the posture signals that alert you to her need.

Accidents Happen

If you see your pup about to eliminate somewhere other than the designated area, interrupt her immediately. Say "wait, wait, wait!" or clap your hands loudly to startle her into stopping. Carry the pup, if she's still small enough, or take her collar and lead her to the correct area. Once your dog is in the potty area, give her the command to eliminate. Use a friendly voice for the command, then wait patiently for her to produce. The pup may be tense because you've just startled her and may have to relax a bit before she's able to eliminate. When she does her job, include the command word in the praise you give ("good potty").

The old-fashioned way of housetraining involved punishing a dog's mistakes even before she knew what she was supposed to do. Puppies were punished for breaking rules they didn't understand about functions they couldn't control. This was not fair. While your dog is new to housetraining, there is no need or excuse for punishing her mistakes. Your job is to take the dog to the potty area just before she needs to go, especially with pups under 3 months old. If you aren't watching your pup closely enough and she has an accident, don't punish the puppy for your failure to anticipate her needs. It's not the pup's fault; it's yours.

In any case, punishment is not an effective tool for housetraining most dogs. Many will react to punishment by hiding puddles and feces where you won't find them right away (like behind the couch or under the desk). This eventually may lead to punishment after the fact, which leads to more hiding, and so on.

Instead of punishing for mistakes, stay a step ahead of potty accidents by learning to anticipate your pup's needs. Accompany your dog to the designated potty area when she needs to go. Tell her what you want her to do and praise her when she goes. This will work wonders. Punishment won't be necessary if you are a good teacher.

What happens if you come upon a mess after the fact? Some trainers say a dog can't remember having eliminated, even a few moments after she has done so. This is not true. The fact is that urine and feces carry a dog's unique scent, which she (and every other dog) can instantly recognize. So, if you happen upon a potty mistake after the fact you can still use it to teach your dog.

But remember, no punishment! Spanking, hitting, shaking, or scaring a puppy for having a housetraining accident is confusing and counterproductive. Spend your energy instead on positive forms of teaching.

Instead of punishing your puppy for mistakes, set her up for success by getting her outside on a regular schedule.

Take your pup and a paper towel to the mess. Point to the urine or feces and calmly tell your puppy, "no potty here." Then scoop or sop up the accident with the paper towel. Take the evidence and the pup to the approved potty area. Drop the mess on the ground and tell the dog, "good potty here," as if she had done the deed in the right place. If your pup sniffs at the evidence, praise her calmly. If the accident happened very recently your dog may not have to go yet, but wait with her a few minutes anyway. If she eliminates, praise her. Afterwards, go finish cleaning up the mess.

Soon the puppy will understand that there is a place where you are pleased about elimination and other places where you are not. Praising for elimination in the approved place will help your pup remember the rules.

Scheduling Basics

With a new puppy in the home, don't be surprised if your rising time is suddenly a little earlier than you've been accustomed to. Puppies have earned a reputation as very early risers. When your pup wakes you at the crack of dawn, you will have to get up and take her to her elimination spot. Be patient. When your dog is an adult, she may enjoy sleeping in as much as you do.

A reasonable schedule will include time when your puppy can be out and about in the house with you. If she's nearby, you can watch her for signs that she needs a potty break.

At the end of this chapter, you'll find a typical housetraining schedule for puppies aged 10 weeks to 6 months. (To find schedules for younger and older pups, and for adult dogs, visit this book's companion web site.) It's fine to adjust the rising times when using this schedule, but you should not adjust the intervals between feedings and potty outings unless your pup's behavior justifies a change. Your puppy can only meet your expectations in housetraining if you help her learn the rules.

The schedule for puppies is devised with the assumption that someone will be home most of the time with the pup. That would be the best scenario, of course, but is not always possible.

Puppies need very frequent trips outside. As they gain physical control and maturity, you won't have to take quite so many walks!

You may be able to ease the problems of a latchkey pup by having a neighbor or friend look in on the pup at noon and take her to eliminate. A better solution might be hiring a pet sitter to drop by midday. A professional pet sitter will be knowledgeable about companion animals and can give your pup high-quality care and socialization. Some can even help train your pup in both potty manners and basic obedience. Ask your veterinarian and your dog-owning friends to recommend a good pet sitter.

If you must leave your pup alone during her early housetraining period, be sure to cover the entire floor of her corral with thick layers of overlapping newspaper. If you come home to messes in the puppy corral, just clean them up. Be patient—she's still a baby.

Use this schedule (and the ones on the companion web site) as a basic plan to help prevent housetraining accidents. Meanwhile, use your own powers of observation to discover how to best modify the basic schedule to fit your dog's unique needs. Each dog is an individual and will have her own rhythms, and each dog is reliable at a different age.

Schedule for Pups 10 Weeks to 6 Months

7:00 a.m.	Get up and take the puppy from her sleeping crate to her potty spot.
7:15	Clean up last night's messes, if any.
7:30	Food and fresh water.
7:45	Pick up the food bowl. Take the pup to her potty spot; wait and praise.
8:00	The pup plays around your feet while you have your breakfast.
9:00	Potty break (younger pups may not be able to wait this long).
9:15	Play and obedience practice.
10:00	Potty break.
10:15	The puppy is in her corral with safe toys to chew and play with.
11:30	Potty break (younger pups may not be able to wait this long).
11:45	Food and fresh water.
12:00 p.m.	Pick up the food bowl and take the pup to her potty spot.
12:15	The puppy is in her corral with safe toys to chew and play with.
1:00	Potty break (younger pups may not be able to wait this long).
1:15	Put the pup on a leash and take her around the house with you.
3:30	Potty break (younger pups may not be able to wait this long).
3:45	Put the pup in her corral with safe toys and chews for solitary play and/or a nap.
4:45	Potty break.
5:00	Food and fresh water.
5:15	Potty break.
5:30	The pup may play nearby (either leashed or in her corral) while you prepare your evening meal.
7:00	Potty break.

7:15	Leashed or closely watched, the pup may play and socialize with family and visitors.
9:15	Potty break (younger pups may not be able to wait this long).
10:45	Last chance to potty.
11:00	Put the pup to bed in her crate for the night.

Learning More About Your Shih Tzu

Some Good Books

About Shih Tzu

Cunliffe, Juliette, *The Complete Shih Tzu,* Ringpress Books, 2000.
Regelman, JoAnn, *A New Owner's Guide to Shih Tzu,* TFH Publications, 1996.
White, Jo Ann, *The Official Book of the Shih Tzu,* TFH Publications, 1997.

Canine Activities

Cecil, Barbara, and Gerianne Darnell, *Competitive Obedience Training for the Small Dog,* T9E Publishing, 1994.

Daniels, Julie, *Enjoying Dog Agility: From Backyard to Competition,* 1991.

Davis, Kathy Diamond, *Therapy Dogs: Training Your Dog to Help Others,* 2nd edition, Dogwise Publications, 2002.

Habgood, Dawn, and Robert Habgood, *Pets on the Go: The Definitive Pet Accommodation and Vacation Guide,* Dawbert Press, 2002.

Mobil Travel Guide, *On the Road With Your Pet,* Mobil Travel Guides, 2004.

Smith, Cheryl S., *The Absolute Beginner's Guide to Showing Your Dog,* Three Rivers Press, 2001.

Volhard, Jack and Wendy, *The Canine Good Citizen: Every Dog Can Be One,* 2nd edition, Howell Book House, 1997.

Health Care

Ackerman, Lowell, *Guide to Skin and Haircoat Problems in Dogs,* Alpine Publications, 1994.

DeBitetto, James, DVM, and Sarah Hodgson, *You and Your Puppy: Training and Health Care for Puppy's First Year,* Howell Book House, 1995.

Giffin, James M., and Liisa D. Carlson. *Dog Owner's Home Veterinary Handbook,* 3rd edition, Howell Book House, 2000.

McGinnis, Terri, DVM, *The Well Dog Book,* Random House, 1996.

Training

Baer, Ted, *Communicating with Your Dog,* Barron's Educational Series, 1999.

Benjamin, Carol Lea, *Dog Training for Kids,* Howell Book House, 1988.

Benjamin, Carol Lea, *Mother Knows Best,* Howell Book House, 1985.

Benjamin, Carol Lea, *Surviving Your Dog's Adolescence,* Howell Book House, 1993.

Evans, Job Michael, *People, Pooches and Problems,* 2nd edition, Howell Book House, 2001.

Hastings, Pat, and Erin Ann Rouse, eds., *Another Piece of the Puzzle: Puppy Development,* Dogfolk Enterprises, 2004.

Kalstone, Shirlee, *How to Housebreak Your Dog in Seven Days,* revised edition, Bantam Books, 2004.

Volhard, Jack, and Melissa Bartlett, *Dog Training for Dummies,* John Wiley & Sons, 2001.

Wrede, Barbara J., *Civilizing Your Puppy,* Barron's Educational Series, 1997.

Clubs and Associations

American Kennel Club

www.akc.org

In addition to the informative main web site, there are special links to AKC affiliates such as Companion Animal Recovery (CAR) and the Canine Health Foundation (CHF). The AKC has released a video on every dog breed, as well as many other informative pamphlets, videos, and books. The AKC library is located at 260 Madison Avenue, New York, NY 10016. Registration matters are handled at 5580 Centerview Drive, Raleigh, NC 27606.

Canadian Kennel Club
www.ckc.ca
This is the registry for purebred dogs in Canada. Like the AKC, it licenses dog shows and other canine events. You can also contact the CKC at 89 Skyway Ave., Suite 100, Etobicoke, Ontario, Canada M9W 6R4.

American Dog Owners Association
www.adoa.org
The American Dog Owners Association combats anti-dog legislation. Their address is 1654 Columbia Turnpike, Castleton, NY 12033.

Delta Society
www.deltasociety.org
The Delta Society promotes the human-animal bond through pet-assisted therapy and other programs. The organization's address is 875 124th Ave. NE, Suite 101, Bellevue, WA 98005.

Therapy Dogs International
www.tdi-dog.org
Therapy Dogs International certifies therapy dogs. The organization's address is 88 Bartley Road, Flanders, NJ 07836.

Shih Tzu Web Sites

American Shih Tzu Club
www.shihtzu.org
This web site contains a wealth of information on all aspects of selecting and living with a Shih Tzu. It includes contact information for local Shih Tzu clubs, breeder referrals, and Shih Tzu rescue groups across the country, and explains how to order a number of breed-specific books, pamphlets, merchandise, and videos.

Shih Tzu Fanciers of Southern California
www.stfsc.bizland.com/
The web site of this club contains a great deal of information on Shih Tzu in agility and Shih Tzu rescue groups.

Shih Tzu Rescue
www.jvars-shihtzu.com/Rescue
Stop by this web site for information on adopting a Shih Tzu from a rescue organization. You can also post your own inspirational rescue story online.

Pet Finder
www.petfinder.com
This is a nationwide all-breed rescue site that may help you in your search for a rescue Shih Tzu.

Shih Tzu Magazine
www.fix.net/~dogmag/shihtzu/shihtzu-home.html
This site for a Shih Tzu magazine includes many articles and information on how to subscribe.

Health Resources

Canine Health Foundation
www.akcchf.org
The AKC Canine Health Foundation funds cutting-edge research into canine diseases.

Canis Major
www.canismajor.com/dog/allergy.html
Lots of information on canine allergies, including an article on human allergies to canines.

Orthopedic Foundation for Animals
www.ofa.org
The Orthopedic Foundation for Animals certifies the soundness of hips and other joints, and maintains a database of dogs who have been certified. They can also be reached at 2300 E. Nifong Blvd., Columbia, MO 65201-3856.

Pet Education
www.peteducation.com
This site contains general veterinary news.

Spay USA
www.spayusa.org
The world's largest low-cost spay-neuter referral program, with more than 900 participants nationwide. The site includes information on why you should spay or neuter your pet. You can also call 1-888-PETS-911 or 1-800-248-SPAY to locate a low-cost facility near you.

Canine Eye Registry Foundation
www.vet.purdue.edu/~yshen/cerf.html
This is the web site of the Canine Eye Registry Foundation (CERF) at Purdue University, which certifies tests on canine eyes. They can also be contacted by telephone at 765-494-8179.

Grooming Supplies and Instructions

Bottle Babies
www.bottlebabies.com
This web site contains several sizes of water bottles and free-standing water bottle holders. Similar items can be ordered from Caravel Products (caraval1@msn.com).

Cherrybrook
www.cherrybrook.com
A good basic dog supply catalogue for such things as crates, hair dryers, grooming tables, exercise pens, and shampoos.

Lainee
www.laineeltd.com
A large selection of latex bands, bows, leads, and other supplies for your Shih Tzu.

Show Off
www.showoffproducts.com
This site offers grooming supplies (including bands, bows, soft pin brushes, and combs) and two grooming videos: one for Shih Tzu in full coat and the other demonstrating various pet clips.

Training Groups

Association of Pet Dog Trainers
www.apdt.com
You can also contact this organization at 5096 Sand Road SE, Iowa City, IA 52240-8217.

American Dog Trainer's Network
www.inch.com
If you click on www.inch.com/~dogs/clicker.html, you'll find a good basic explanation of clicker training.

National Association of Dog Obedience Instructors
www.nadoi.org
You can also contact this organization at PMB 369, 729 Grapevine Highway, Hurst, TX 76054-2085.

Out and About With Your Shih Tzu

Infodog
www.infodog.com
This is a good site for locating AKC-licensed dog shows and obedience or agility trials in your area. It also has links to rescue organizations nationwide.

Travel Dog
www.traveldog.com
Lots of information on where you and your dog will be welcome when you travel.

Photo Credits:
Kent Dannen: 1, 4–5, 15, 17, 19, 24, 28, 29, 34, 35, 37, 48, 55, 56, 67 (bottom), 68, 74, 76, 77, 85, 87, 92, 96, 98–99, 126, 129
Jeannie Harrison: 8–9, 13, 32, 33, 38–39, 40, 41, 45, 47, 49, 50, 52, 53, 59, 64, 66, 75, 82, 83 (top), 90, 100, 120, 122, 124, 127, 128, 130, 131
Richard Lawall: 11, 21, 27, 57, 60, 62, 63, 65, 67 (top), 83 (bottom)

Index